ABOUT THE EDITOR

SIMON VAN BOOY is the author of *The Secret Lives of People in Love* and *Love Begins in Winter*, which in 2009 won the Frank O'Connor International Short Story Award. He has written for *The New York Times*, *The Daily Telegraph*, *The Times*, *The Guardian*, and NPR. He lives in New York City where he lectures at the School of Visual Arts and is involved in the Rutgers Early College Humanities program for young adults living in under-served communities. His work has been translated into nine different languages.

ALSO BY SIMON VAN BOOY

WHY OUR DECISIONS DON'T MATTER

Edited by Simon Van Booy

HARPER**PERENNIAL** ⬤ MODERN**THOUGHT**

NEW YORK • LONDON • TORONTO • SYDNEY • NEW DELHI • AUCKLAND

HARPER**PERENNIAL** ● MODERN**THOUGHT**

HarperCollins books may be purchased for educational, business, or sales promotional use. For information, please write: Special Markets Department, HarperCollins Publishers, 10 East 53rd Street, New York, NY 10022.

FIRST EDITION

Designed by Justin Dodd

Library of Congress Cataloging-in-Publication data is available upon request.

ISBN 978-0-06-184555-0

10 11 12 13 14 OV/RRD 10 9 8 7 6 5 4 3 2 1

To my daughter, Madeleine:
No decision you could ever make
would stop me from loving you

CONTENTS

PREFACE TO THE SERIES

My hope for these books is to present interesting and exciting philosophical ideas in a straightforward, but intelligent, language that can be understood by everyone. I believe that philosophy is a subject we have a natural gift for, but a subject often regarded as one with no practical value—and closed to anyone outside the walls of universities. I am committed to the idea that these central questions of life are part of our everyday lives—that we all possess the skill and agility to tackle them, and that by pondering them, we can experience more fulfillment in our relationships, in our work, and in how we view ourselves.

Inside these books are readings, poems, quotations, and visual images that will inspire you to continue exploring the subject for years to come. I have tried my best to present philosophical ideas with no immediate resolution as immediately accessible for everyday thinking.

These volumes are not meant to convince you of anything, to be a definitive source, or to offer any new insights on a topic. Their purpose is simply to introduce you to an age-old theme that quite possibly has already taken a key role in your life.

To begin then, let me tell you about a small statue I once saw in a New Orleans public park. The young man of marble who stood before me (discolored by years of affection from birds) was holding a book to his heart with one hand, while using his other hand to pick a grape from a vine.

If the grape were to represent life, and the book over his heart, knowledge, then one interpretation may be that book learning and actual life experience complement each other. So by reading about other people's experiences in this book, we may begin to understand ourselves with fresh insight. Reading reassures us that no matter how alone we might feel, there are many others—spread as wide as history itself— who have felt the same way we have, who have occupied the rooms we find ourselves locked in at various points of our lives.

One celebrated aspect of literature is that unlike the ambitious exactitude of science, literature is often ambiguous—meaning that two people might have very different ideas about what a play, poem, or book is about. While at first this implied vagueness might seem detrimental to literature, it's one of its sustaining virtues, and allows people from different cultures, and even different time periods, to learn something about their own lives from a single story. If a story were viewed as a literal history, one could argue that it wouldn't be quite as useful—because history is traditionally viewed as a record of what we think happened, whereas story and myth are more like advice whispered to us by a wise grandmother. Many of the great geniuses who lived over the last five thousand years were not writers at all, but oral storytellers who left it up to others to write down what they said.

Stories, parables, and dialogues were their preferred method of teaching—in other words, instead of saying to a lazy child: "Go tidy your room now!" our greatest thinkers would probably have begun with something like: "There was once a girl who never tidied her room . . ."

INTRODUCTION

From the moment you wake up in the morning, there are decisions to be made. What should you eat for breakfast? What will you wear? What plans will you make for the weekend?

Everyday decisions give us the idea that we are in control of our own lives. But there are also far more difficult decisions. Should you divorce your current partner? Should you take that job overseas? Should you own up to something and face the penalty, or live with a sense of guilt? Should you allow surgeons to operate on your child, or seek other, less invasive ways to fix a potentially threatening condition?

In light of these more challenging decisions, the premise for this paradoxically titled book may seem at first to be utterly ridiculous, especially if we feel the fate of loved ones depends on us making what we perceive to be the *right* decision.

This book is an introduction to a very old theme, and supposes that our tiny, daily decisions about what to have for lunch are as utterly meaningless as those we perceive are critical to our lives and those in our care.

WHY OUR DECISIONS
DON'T MATTER

Jack Kerouac is considered a leading figure of the American Beat Generation. The Beats rejected the traditional postwar idea of success through commercial prosperity and instead pursued their own ideas of freedom and enlightenment through jazz, cross-country road trips, drugs, alcohol, sex, love, and the natural world. Kerouac's most famous novel is *On the Road*, published in the United States in 1957. The book was typed on a continuous roll of paper (120 feet long) in three weeks. The story of Dean Moriarty and Sal Paradise continues to inspire generations of Americans in their quest for national and personal identity. Jack Kerouac died in 1969, at age forty-seven.

The first reading is from one of Kerouac's lesser-known works, *Book of Haikus*, in which Kerouac explores this Japanese poetic form. The haiku that follows suggests that no matter what we decide to do, life sometimes happens outside of our control.

Jack Kerouac

"Missing a Kick" from *Book of Haikus*

Missing a kick
at the icebox door
It closed anyway.

Sophocles was born in 496 BCE, died in 406 BCE and was greatly admired in his own time, holding positions in the military, government, and religious institutions. Sophocles also acted in the theater and was known for his musical skill and comedic dexterity with props. Although he wrote over one hundred plays, only a handful have survived, including *Oedipus Rex*, in which Oedipus is fated by the gods to grow up and kill his father, then marry his mother. Despite extreme measures to avoid this from happening, the prophecy is eventually fulfilled, and Oedipus learns that he is the murderer that he has been seeking, and that his wife is also his birth mother.

Even though Oedipus's hubris (excessive pride) may have contributed to his grisly fate, the Greeks at this time may have lived with the idea that much of what happens in our lives, is not within our power to change.

In the following excerpt from *Oedipus Rex*, we join Oedipus on the verge of his gruesome discovery.

Sophocles

from *Oedipus Rex*

OEDIPUS

Elders, if I, who never yet before
Have met the man, may make a guess, methinks
I see the herdsman who we long have sought;
His time-worn aspect matches with the years
Of yonder aged messenger; besides
I seem to recognize the men who bring him
As servants of my own. But you, perchance,
Having in past days known or seen the herd,
May better by sure knowledge my surmise.

CHORUS

I recognize him; one of Laius' house;
A simple hind, but true as any man. (ENTER HERDSMAN.)

OEDIPUS

Corinthian, stranger, I address thee first,
Is this the man thou meanest!

MESSENGER

This is he.

SIMON VAN BOOY

OEDIPUS

And now old man, look up and answer all

I ask thee. Wast thou once of Laius' house?

HERDSMAN

I was, a thrall, not purchased but home-bred.

OEDIPUS

What was thy business? how wast thou employed?

HERDSMAN

The best part of my life I tended sheep.

OEDIPUS

What were the pastures thou didst most frequent?

HERDSMAN

Cithaeron and the neighboring alps.

OEDIPUS

Then there

Thou must have known yon man, at least by fame?

HERDSMAN

Yon man? in what way? what man dost thou mean?

OEDIPUS

The man here, having met him in past times . . .

HERDSMAN

Off-hand I cannot call him well to mind.

MESSENGER

No wonder, master. But I will revive
His blunted memories. Sure he can recall
What time together both we drove our flocks,
He two, I one, on the Cithaeron range,
For three long summers; I his mate from spring
Till rose Arcturus; then in winter time
I led mine home, he his to Laius' folds.
Did these things happen as I say, or no?

HERDSMAN

'Tis long ago, but all thou say'st is true.

MESSENGER

Well, thou must then remember giving me
A child to rear as my own foster-son?

HERDSMAN

Why dost thou ask this question? What of that?

MESSENGER

Friend, he that stands before thee was that child.

HERDSMAN

A plague upon thee! Hold thy wanton tongue!

OEDIPUS

Softly, old man, rebuke him not; thy words
Are more deserving chastisement than his.

HERDSMAN

O best of masters, what is my offense?

OEDIPUS

Not answering what he asks about the child.

HERDSMAN

He speaks at random, babbles like a fool.

OEDIPUS

If thou lack'st grace to speak, I'll loose thy tongue.

HERDSMAN

For mercy's sake abuse not an old man.

OEDIPUS

Arrest the villain, seize and pinion him!

HERDSMAN

Alack, alack!
What have I done? what wouldst thou further learn?

OEDIPUS

Didst give this man the child of whom he asks?

HERDSMAN

I did; and would that I had died that day!

OEDIPUS

And die thou shalt unless thou tell the truth.

HERDSMAN

But, if I tell it, I am doubly lost.

OEDIPUS

The knave methinks will still prevaricate.

HERDSMAN

Nay, I confessed I gave it long ago.

OEDIPUS

Whence came it? was it thine, or given to thee?

HERDSMAN

I had it from another, 'twas not mine.

OEDIPUS

From whom of these our townsmen, and what house?

HERDSMAN

Forbear for God's sake, master, ask no more.

OEDIPUS

If I must question thee again, thou'rt lost.

HERDSMAN

Well then—it was a child of Laius' house.

OEDIPUS

Slave-born or one of Laius' own race?

HERDSMAN

Ah me!
I stand upon the perilous edge of speech.

OEDIPUS

And I of hearing, but I still must hear.

HERDSMAN

Know then the child was by repute his own,

But she within, thy consort best could tell.

OEDIPUS

What! she, she gave it thee?

HERDSMAN

'Tis so, my king.

OEDIPUS

With what intent?

HERDSMAN

To make away with it.

OEDIPUS

What, she its mother.

HERDSMAN

Fearing a dread weird.

SIMON VAN BOOY

OEDIPUS

What weird?

HERDSMAN

'Twas told that he should slay his sire.

OEDIPUS

What didst thou give it then to this old man?

HERDSMAN

Through pity, master, for the babe. I thought
He'd take it to the country whence he came;
But he preserved it for the worst of woes.
For if thou art in sooth what this man saith,
God pity thee! thou wast to misery born.

OEDIPUS

Ah me! ah me! all brought to pass, all true!
O light, may I behold thee nevermore!
I stand a wretch, in birth, in wedlock cursed,
A parricide, incestuously, triply cursed! (EXIT OEDIPUS.)

CHORUS (STROPHE 1)

Races of mortal man
Whose life is but a span,

I count ye but the shadow of a shade!
For he who most doth know
Of bliss, hath but the show;
A moment, and the visions pale and fade.
Thy fall, O Oedipus, thy piteous fall
Warns me none born of women blest to call.

(ANTISTROPHE 1)

For he of marksmen best,
O Zeus, outshot the rest,
And won the prize supreme of wealth and power.
By him the vulture maid
Was quelled, her witchery laid;
He rose our savior and the land's strong tower.
We hailed thee king and from that day adored
Of mighty Thebes the universal lord.

(STROPHE 2)

O heavy hand of fate!
Who now more desolate,
Whose tale more sad than thine, whose lot more dire?
O Oedipus, discrowned head,
Thy cradle was thy marriage bed;

One harborage sufficed for son and sire.
How could the soil thy father eared so long
Endure to bear in silence such a wrong?

(ANTISTROPHE 2)

All-seeing Time hath caught
Guilt, and to justice brought
The son and sire commingled in one bed.
O child of Laius' ill-starred race
Would I had ne'er beheld thy face;
I raise for thee a dirge as o'er the dead.
Yet, sooth to say, through thee I drew new breath,
And now through thee I feel a second death.

That which God writes on thy forehead, thou wilt come to it.

—The Koran

Born around 50 BCE, Epictetus was the sort of philosopher who valued usefulness above anything else, and believed sincerely in helping people live more fulfilling lives. His commonsense approach to ideas may account for his enduring appeal, and he spent his life committed to the idea that philosophy could improve a person's everyday existence. Although Epictetus was born a slave, his master was so impressed with his intellectual capability that he sent him to study in Rome, which led to his eventual emancipation. Later in life, he taught at a philosophical school that he opened on the northwest coast of Greece.

In modern society, many people experience despair, unhappiness, and worry over things that are simply not within their power to change. In *The Art of Living*, Epictetus addresses the idea that in some ways, our decisions don't matter—because so much of life takes place outside of our control.

Epictetus

from *The Art of Living*

Happiness and freedom begin with a clear understanding of one principle: Some things are within our control, and some things are not. It is only after you have faced up to this fundamental rule and learned to distinguish between what you can and can't control that inner tranquility and outer effectiveness become possible.

Within our control are our own opinions, aspirations, desires, and the things that repel us. These areas are quite rightly our concern, because they are directly subject to our influence. We always have a choice about the contents and character of our inner lives.

Outside our control, however, are such things as what kind of body we have, whether we're born into wealth or strike it rich, how we are regarded by others, and our status in society. We must remember that those things are externals and are therefore not our concern. Trying to control or to change what we can't only results in torment.

Remember: The things within our power are naturally at our disposal, free from any restraint or hindrance; but those things outside our power are weak, dependent, or determined by the whims and actions of others. Remember, too, that if you think that you have free rein over things that are

SIMON VAN BOOY

naturally beyond your control, or if you attempt to adopt the affairs of others as your own, your pursuits will be thwarted and you will become a frustrated, anxious, and fault-finding person.

Like many ancient poets, prophets, and philosophers, Homer never actually wrote anything down. He orally composed two poems, the *Iliad* and the *Odyssey* around 850 BCE.

The *Odyssey* and the *Iliad* were once considered to have religious significance, and the ancient Greeks may have turned to them as guides to learn about the gods and how people should behave.

The *Odyssey* is considered to be one of the most important stories in human history. Although the way of life in the poem is thousands of years old, many people believe that this epic work explores very modern problems.

In this extract from Homer's *Odyssey*, the action takes place while Odysseus and his crew are trying to get home. According to an underworld prophet who consulted with Odysseus, to reach their home of Ithaka they must sail through an area inhabited by Skylla, a six-headed monster, who randomly selects members of the crew for her afternoon snack. Those who manage to survive Skylla may still perish by way of a giant whirlpool that exists on the other side of Skylla's lair.

Homer

from *The Odyssey of Homer*

"But of the two rocks, one reaches up into the wide heaven

with a pointed peak, and a dark cloud stands always

around it,

75 and never at any time draws away from it, nor does the

sunlight

ever hold that peak, either in the early or the late summer,

nor could any man who was mortal climb there, or stand

mounted

on the summit, not if he had twenty hands and twenty

feet, for the rock goes sherly up, as if it were polished.

80 Halfway up the cliff there is a cave, misty-looking

and turned toward Erebos and the dark, the very direction

from which, O shining Odysseus, you and your men will be

steering

your hollow ship; and from the hollow ship no vigorous

young man with a bow could shoot to the hole in the

cliffside.

85 In that cavern Skylla lives, whose howling is terror.

Her voice indeed is only as loud as a new-born puppy

could make, but she herself is an evil monster. No one,

not even a god encountering her, could be glad at that sight.

She has twelve feet, and all of them wave in the air. She has six

SIMON VAN BOOY

90   necks upon her, grown to great length, and upon each neck

there is a horrible head, with teeth in it, set in three rows

close together and stiff, full of black death. Her body

from the waist down is holed up inside the hollow cavern,

but she holds her heads poked out and away from the

       terrible hollow,

95   and there she fishes, peering all over the cliffside, looking

for dolphins or dogfish to catch or anything bigger,

some sea monster, of whom Amphitrite keeps so many;

never can sailors boast aloud that their ship has passed her

without any loss of men, for with each of her heads she

       snatches

100   one man away and carries him off from the dark-prowed

       vessel.

"The other cliff is lower; you will see it, Odysseus,

for they lie close together, you could even cast with an arrow

across. There is a great fig tree grows there, dense with foliage,

and under this shining Charybdis sucks down the black water.

105   For three times a day she flows it up, and three times she

       sucks it

terribly down; may you not be there when she sucks down

       water,

for not even the Earthshaker could rescue you out of that

       evil.

But sailing your ship swiftly drive her past and avoid her,

and make for Skylla's rock instead, since it is far better

110   to mourn six friends lost out of your ship than the whole

company."

So she spoke, but I in turn said to her in answer:

"Come then, goddess, answer me truthfully this: is there

some way for me to escape away from deadly Charybdis,

but yet fight the other one off, when she attacks my

companions?"

115   So I spoke, and she, shining among goddesses, answered:

"Hardy man, your mind is full forever of fighting

and battle work. Will you not give way even to the

immortals?

She is no mortal thing but a mischief immortal, dangerous

difficult and bloodthirsty, and there is no fighting against her,

120   nor any force of defense. It is best to run away from her.

For if you arm for battle beside her rock and waste time

there, I fear she will make another outrush and catch you

with all her heads, and snatch away once more the same number

of men. Drive by as hard as you can, but invoke Krataiïs.

125   She is the mother of Skylla and bore this mischief for

mortals,

and she will stay her from making another sally against you.

"Then you will reach the island Thrinakia, where are pastured

the cattle and the fat sheep of the sun god, Helios,

seven herds of oxen, and as many beautiful sheepflocks,

130   and fifty to each herd. There is no giving birth among them,
      nor do they ever die away, and their shepherdesses
      are gods, nymphs with sweet hair, Lampetia and Phaethousa,
      whom shining Neaira bore to Hyperion the sun god.
      These, when their queenly mother had given them birth and
            reared them,
135   she settled in the island Thrinakia, far away, to live
      there and guard their father's sheep and his horn-curved
            cattle.
      Then, if you keep your mind on homecoming and leave these
            unharmed,
      you might all make your way to Ithaka, after much suffering;
      but if you do harm them, then I testify to the destruction
140   of your ship and your companions, but if you yourself get
            clear,
      you will come home in bad case with the loss of all your
            companions."
      So she spoke, and Dawn of the golden throne came on us.
      She, shining among goddesses, went away, up the island.
      Then, going back on board my ship, I told my companions
145   also to go aboard, and to cast off the stern cables,
      and quickly they went aboard the ship and sat to the
            oarlocks,
      and sitting well in order dashed the oars in the gray sea;
      but fair-haired Circe, the dread goddess who talks with

mortals,
sent us an excellent companion, a following wind, filling
150   the sails, to carry from astern the ship with the dark prow.
We ourselves, over all the ship making fast the running gear,
sat there, and let the wind and the steersman hold her
      steady.
Then, sorrowful as I was, I spoke and told my companions:
"Friends, since it is not right for one or two of us only
155   to know the divinations that Circe, bright among goddesses,
gave me, so I will tell you, and knowing all we may either
die, or turn aside from death and escape destruction.
First of all she tells us to keep away from the magical
Sirens and their singing and their flowery meadow, but only
160   I, she said, was to listen to them, but you must tie me
hard in hurtful bonds, to hold me fast in position
upright against the mast, with the ropes' ends fastened
      around it;
but if I supplicate you and implore you to set me
free, then you must tie me fast with even more lashings."
165   So as I was telling all the details to my companions,
meanwhile the well-made ship was coming rapidly closer
to the Sirens' isle, for the harmless wind was driving her
      onward;
but immediately then the breeze dropped, and a windless
calm fell there, and some divinity stilled the tossing

SIMON VAN BOOY

170 waters. My companions stood up, and took the sails down,
and stowed them away in the hollow hull, and took their
places
for rowing, and with their planed oarblades whitened the
water.
Then I, taking a great wheel of wax, with the sharp bronze
cut a little piece off, and rubbed it together in my heavy
175 hands, and soon the wax grew softer, under the powerful
stress of the sun, and the heat and light of Hyperion's
lordling.
One after another, I stopped the ears of all my companions,
and they then bound me hand and foot in the fast ship,
standing
upright against the mast with the ropes' ends lashed
around it,
180 and sitting then to row they dashed their oars in the
gray sea.
But when we were as far from the land as a voice shouting
carries, lightly plying, the swift ship as it drew nearer
was seen by the Sirens, and they directed their sweet song
toward us:
"Come this way, honored Odysseus, great glory of the
Achaians,
185 and stay your ship, so that you can listen here to our singing;
for no one else has ever sailed past this place in his black ship

until he has listened to the honey-sweet voice that issues

from our lips; then goes on, well pleased, knowing more than
ever

he did; for we know everything that the Argives and Trojans

190   did and suffered in wide Troy through the gods' despite.

Over all the generous earth we know everything that
happens."

So they sang, in sweet utterance, and the heart within me

desired to listen, and I signaled my companions to set me

free, nodding with my brows, but they leaned on and rowed hard,

195   and Perimedes and Eurylochos, rising up, straightway

fastened me with even more lashings and squeezed me
tighter.

But when they had rowed on past the Sirens, and we could
no longer

hear their voices and lost the sound of their singing,
presently

my eager companions took away from their ears the
beeswax

200   with which I had stopped them. Then they set me free from
my lashings.

But after we had left the island behind, the next thing

we saw was smoke, and a heavy surf, and we heard it
thundering.

The men were terrified, and they let the oars fall out of

their hands, and these banged all about in the wash. The ship stopped

205 still, with the men no longer rowing to keep way on her.
Then I going up and down the ship urged on my companions,
standing beside each man and speaking to him in kind words:
"Dear friends, surely we are not unlearned in evils.
This is no greater evil now than it was when the Cyclops

210 had us cooped in his hollow cave by force and violence,
but even there, by my courage and counsel and my intelligence,
we escaped away. I think that all this will be remembered
some day too. Then do as I say, let us all be won over.
Sit well, all of you, to your oarlocks, and dash your oars deep

215 into the breaking surf of the water, so in that way Zeus
might grant that we get clear of this danger and flee away from it.
For you, steersman, I have this order; so store it deeply
in your mind, as you control the steering oar of this hollow
ship; you must keep her clear from where the smoke and the breakers

220 are, and make hard for the sea rock lest, without your knowing,
she might drift that way, and you bring all of us into disaster."
So I spoke, and they quickly obeyed my words. I had not

spoken yet of Skylla, a plague that could not be dealt with,

for fear my companions might be terrified and give over

225   their rowing, and take cover inside the ship. For my part,

I let go from my mind the difficult instruction that Circe

had given me, for she told me not to be armed for combat;

but I put on my glorious armor and, taking up two long

spears in my hands, I stood bestriding the vessel's foredeck

230   at the prow, for I expected Skylla of the rocks to appear first

from that direction, she who brought pain to my companions.

I could not make her out anywhere, and my eyes grew weary

from looking everywhere on the misty face of the sea rock.

So we sailed up the narrow strait lamenting. On one side

235   was Skylla, and on the other side was shining Charybdis,

who made her terrible ebb and flow of the sea's water.

When she vomited it up, like a caldron over a strong fire,

the whole sea would boil up in turbulence, and the foam flying

spattered the pinnacles of the rocks in either direction;

240   but when in turn again she sucked down the sea's salt water,

the turbulence showed all the inner sea, and the rock around it

groaned terribly, and the ground showed at the sea's bottom,

black with sand; and green fear seized upon my companions.

We in fear of destruction kept our eyes on Charybdis,

245   but meanwhile Skylla out of the hollow vessel snatched six

of my companions, the best of them for strength and hands'

work,

and when I turned to look at the ship, with my other

    companions,

I saw their feet and hands from below, already lifted

high above me, and they cried out to me and called me

250 by name, the last time they ever did it, in heart's sorrow.

And as a fisherman with a very long rod, on a jutting

rock, will cast his treacherous bait for the little fishes,

and sinks the horn of a field-ranging ox into the water,

then hauls them up and throws them on the dry land,

    gasping

255 and struggling, so they gasped and struggled as they were

    hoisted

up the cliff. Right in her doorway she ate them up. They were

    screaming

and reaching out their hands to me in this horrid encounter.

That was the most pitiful scene that these eyes have

    looked on

in my sufferings as I explored the routes over the water.

In the midst of life we are in death.

—The Book of Common Prayer

These next two paintings explore the idea of memento mori, a Latin expression that means:

Remember you are going to die!

"Et in arcadia ego" is an ambiguous Latin phrase addressing roughly the same idea as "memento mori." The skull in Guercino's painting, upon which it is written, once belonged to a person who lived in the mythical land of Arcadia, and enjoyed all the carefree pleasures that the living people in the picture (and presumably the viewer) are currently in the midst of.

The literal idea behind these paintings is to remind people that one day they will die and to appreciate the present moment. However, another reading of these images suggests that while our decisions essentially don't matter due to our mortal fate, by constantly being reminded of this, we are less likely to waste our lives by making decisions that don't grant us a deeper satisfaction. In other words, our decisions don't matter until we realize they don't matter.

Philippe de Champaigne, *Vanitas,* c. 1671

Guercino (Giovanni Francesco Barbieri), *Et in Arcadia Ego*,
c. 1628

It was in the reign of George III

that the above-named personages

lived and quarreled; good or bad,

handsome or ugly, rich or poor,

they are all equal now.

> — *William Makepeace Thackeray from*
> The Memoirs of Barry Lyndon, Esq.

Jorge Luis Borges was a prolific Argentinean poet, writer, speaker, and essayist. Born in Buenos Aires in 1899, Borges began writing books in his early twenties, and as a teacher he encouraged students not to concentrate on literary critics but to focus on actual literature. He went blind in his fifties but continued to write and give lectures. Very much like his father, Borges was committed to social justice. He died in 1986.

This short Borges poem deftly explores how our mortal destiny somehow negates the lofty importance so often bestowed upon the art of decision making.

Jorge Luis Borges

"To Whoever Is Reading Me"

You are invulnerable. Have they not granted you,

those powers that preordain your destiny,

the certainty of dust? Is not your time

as irreversible as that same river

where Heraclitus, mirrored, saw the symbol

of fleeting life? A marble slab awaits you

which you will not read—on it, already written,

the date, the city, and the epitaph.

Other men too are only dreams of time,

not indestructible bronze or burnished gold;

the universe is, like you, a Proteus.

Dark, you will enter the darkness that awaits you,

doomed to the limits of your traveled time.

Know that in some sense you are already dead.

SIMON VAN BOOY

The fear of death follows from the fear of life. A man who lives fully is prepared to die at any time.

—*Mark Twain*

Rembrandt Van Rijn was born in the Netherlands in 1606 and is considered a major figure in Western art, largely because of his extreme talent for contrasting light and dark (a technique referred to as "chiaroscuro"). He was, for a time, the leading portrait painter in Holland and is perhaps most famous for capturing the emotional nuances of his subjects. Rembrandt's personal life was marked with tragedy; three of his four children died in infancy, and his wife died eight years into the marriage at the age of thirty. Rembrandt died in Amsterdam twenty-seven years later.

In the first self-portrait, the artist is thirty-four years old. In the second, he is sixty-three years old and only months away from death. When the paintings are hung next to each other, they remind us how quickly life passes.

Rembrandt Van Rijn, *Self Portrait at the Age of 34,* 1640

Rembrandt Van Rijn, *Self Portrait at the Age of 63*, 1669

Horace was born in 65 BCE, the son of an emancipated slave. Horace's father invested a great deal of money educating his son and sent him to Athens to study Greek and philosophy. After Julius Caesar was assassinated on March 15, 44 BCE, Horace became a soldier under Brutus, and saw combat at the Battle of Philippi. Returning to Italy under an amnesty for all who had fought against the victorious Augustus, Horace discovered that his estate had been confiscated and that he was destitute. Somehow, he managed to secure work as a treasurer and live the rest of his life in comfort, while continuing to write at a farm given to him by his mentor and friend, Maecenas. Both men died the same year in 8 BCE.

The next reading comes from *The Odes of Horace* and is the source of the well-known dictum *carpe diem*, often translated as "seize the day." The idea behind carpe diem is that one day we will die, and therefore we should enjoy life while we still have breath to do so.

Horace

The Odes of Horace, *Book 1.11, 23 BCE*

Tu ne quaesieris, scire nefas, quem mihi, quem tibi

finem di dederint, Leuconoe, nec Babylonios

temptaris numeros. ut melius, quidquid erit, pati.

seu pluris hiemes seu tribuit Iuppiter ultimam,

quae nunc oppositis debilitat pumicibus mare

Tyrrhenum: sapias, vina liques et spatio brevi

spem longam reseces. dum loquimur, fugerit invida

aetas: carpe diem quam minimum credula postero.

I pray you not, Leuconoe, to pore

With unpermitted eyes on what may be

Appointed by the gods for you and me,

Nor on Chaldean figures any more.

'T were infinitely better to implore

The present only: —whether Jove decree

More winters yet to come, or whether he

Make even this, whose hard, wave-eaten shore

Shatters the Tuscan seas to-day, the last—

Be wise withal, and rack your wine, nor fill

Your bosom with large hopes; for while I sing,

The envious close of time is narrowing;—

SIMON VAN BOOY

So seize the day,—or ever it be past,—

And let the morrow come for what it will.

—Translated from the Latin by John Conington

And behold joy and gladness, slaying oxen, and killing sheep, eating flesh, and drinking wine: let us eat and drink; for to morrow we shall die.

—*Isaiah 22:13*

Ah, the knowledge of impermanence that haunts our days is their very fragrance.

—*Rainer Maria Rilke*

Emily Dickinson was born in 1830 to a prosperous family in Amherst, Massachusetts. The Dickinson house was alight with ambition, both legal and political; however, the world of her father was not one Dickinson took much interest in. She preferred gardening, baking, reading, playing the piano, and taking walks. Despite a single year at a female seminary and the occasional trip to Boston to see an optician—she barely left Amherst.

When she died in her mid-fifties, she left behind almost two thousand poems, only a few of which were published during her lifetime. In the following poem, Dickinson encourages the reader to view himself as someone completely unimportant, and therefore free from a preconceived idea of self-worth. Once the reader is free from being "somebody," he is free to enjoy the gentle beauty of wherever he is at that moment. If one has nothing, perhaps the only remaining luxury is freedom. In realizing that you are nobody and your decisions don't matter, you are free to wander the world in awe of everything, unhindered by the need to make judgments or comparisons.

Emily Dickinson

"I'm Nobody! Who Are You?"

I'm Nobody! Who are you?

Are you—Nobody—too?

Then there's a pair of us?

Don't tell! they'd advertise—you know!

How dreary—to be—Somebody!

How public—like a Frog—

To tell one's name—the livelong June—

To an admiring Bog!

Born in 1694, Jean Marie Arouet de Voltaire (born simply François Marie Arouet) is the most famous writer and philosopher of the European Englightenment. During his eighty-three years of life, he wrote more than twenty thousand letters and many books, plays, and pamphlets. His satirical attacks on the Church and members of the aristocracy led to his imprisonment, but once there, this popular thinker dined frequently with the prison governor. When Voltaire was released from prison, the play he wrote while incarcerated was performed to great success. That same year, Voltaire almost died of smallpox, but claims to have saved himself by "drinking two hundred pints of lemonade."

He died in 1778 shortly after returning to Paris for the production of his final play, at which he met Benjamin Franklin. Although the Archbishop of Paris refused Voltaire a religious burial, his friends smuggled his disguised corpse to an abbey on the outskirts of the city.

Doctor Pangloss, one of the principal characters of Voltaire's most famous novel, *Candide*, believes that "we live in the best of all possible worlds," and that the world is perfect because God is perfect and would not make an imperfect world. Therefore, everything that happens is for the best.

Jean Marie Arouet de Voltaire

from *Candide*

A Tempest, a Shipwreck, an Earthquake, and What Else Befell
Dr. Pangloss, Candide, and James, the Anabaptist

One half of the passengers, weakened and half-dead with the
inconceivable anxiety and sickness which the rolling of a vessel
at sea occasions through the whole human frame, were lost to
all sense of the danger that surrounded them. The others made
loud outcries, or betook themselves to their prayers; the sails
were blown into shreds, and the masts were brought by the
board. The vessel was a total wreck. Everyone was busily employed, but nobody could be either heard or obeyed. The Anabaptist, being upon deck, lent a helping hand as well as the rest,
when a brutish sailor gave him a blow and laid him speech-
less; but, not withstanding, with the violence of the blow the
tar himself tumbled headforemost overboard, and fell upon a
piece of the broken mast, which he immediately grasped.

Honest James, forgetting the injury he had so lately received from him, flew to his assistance, and, with great dif-
ficulty, hauled him in again, but, not withstanding, in the
attempt, was, by a sudden jerk of the ship, thrown overboard
himself, in sight of the very fellow whom he had risked his life
to save and who took not the least notice of him in this distress.

SIMON VAN BOOY

Candide, who beheld all that passed and saw his benefactor one moment rising above water, and the next swallowed up by the merciless waves, was preparing to jump after him, but was prevented by the philosopher Pangloss, who demonstrated to him that the roadstead of Lisbon had been made on purpose for the Anabaptist to be drowned there. While he was proving his argument a priori, the ship foundered, and the whole crew perished, except Pangloss, Candide, and the sailor who had been the means of drowning the good Anabaptist. The villain swam ashore; but Pangloss and Candide reached the land upon a plank.

As soon as they had recovered from their surprise and fatigue they walked towards Lisbon; with what little money they had left they thought to save themselves from starving after having escaped drowning.

Scarcely had they ceased to lament the loss of their benefactor and set foot in the city, when they perceived that the earth trembled under their feet, and the sea, swelling and foaming in the harbor, was dashing in pieces the vessels that were riding at anchor. Large sheets of flames and cinders covered the streets and public places; the houses tottered, and were tumbled topsy-turvy even to their foundations, which were themselves destroyed, and thirty thousand inhabitants of both sexes, young and old, were buried beneath the ruins.

The sailor, whistling and swearing, cried, "Damn it, there's something to be got here."

"What can be the sufficing reason of this phenomenon?" said Pangloss.

"It is certainly the day of judgment," said Candide.

The sailor, defying death in the pursuit of plunder, rushed into the midst of the ruin, where he found some money, with which he got drunk, and, after he had slept himself sober he purchased the favors of the first good-natured wench that came in his way, amidst the ruins of demolished houses and the groans of half-buried and expiring persons.

Pangloss pulled him by the sleeve. "Friend," said he, "this is not right, you trespass against the universal reason, and have mistaken your time."

"Death and zounds!" answered the other, "I am a sailor and was born at Batavia, and have trampled four times upon the crucifix in as many voyages to Japan; you have come to a good hand with your universal reason."

In the meantime, Candide, who had been wounded by some pieces of stone that fell from the houses, lay stretched in the street, almost covered with rubbish.

"For God's sake," said he to Pangloss, "get me a little wine and oil! I am dying."

"This concussion of the earth is no new thing," said Pangloss, "the city of Lima in South America experienced the same last year; the same cause, the same effects; there is certainly a train of sulphur all the way underground from Lima to Lisbon."

"Nothing is more probable," said Candide; "but for the love of God a little oil and wine."

"Probable!" replied the philosopher, "I maintain that the thing is demonstrable."

Candide fainted away, and Pangloss fetched him some water from a neighboring spring. The next day, in searching among the ruins, they found some eatables with which they repaired their exhausted strength. After this they assisted the inhabitants in relieving the distressed and wounded. Some, whom they had humanely assisted, gave them as good a dinner as could be expected under such terrible circumstances. The repast, indeed, was mournful, and the company moistened their bread with their tears; but Pangloss endeavored to comfort them under this affliction by affirming that things could not be otherwise that they were.

"For," said he, "all this is for the very best end, for if there is a volcano at Lisbon it could be in no other spot; and it is impossible but things should be as they are, for everything is for the best."

By the side of the preceptor sat a little man dressed in black, who was one of the familiars of the Inquisition. This person, taking him up with great complaisance, said, "Possibly, my good sir, you do not believe in original sin; for, if everything is best, there could have been no such thing as the fall or punishment of man."

"Your Excellency will pardon me," answered Pangloss, still more politely; "for the fall of man and the curse consequent thereupon necessarily entered into the system of the best of worlds."

"That is as much as to say, sir," rejoined the familiar, "you do not believe in free will."

"Your Excellency will be so good as to excuse me," said Pangloss, "free will is consistent with absolute necessity; for it was necessary we should be free, for in that the will—"

Pangloss was in the midst of his proposition, when the familiar beckoned to his attendant to help him to a glass of port wine.

Bertrand Russell was born in 1872 and orphaned at age three. He was brought up by his grandmother, and then in 1890, admitted to Trinity College, Cambridge, where he earned a first class degree with distinction in philosophy. He wrote *The Principles of Mathematics* in 1903 and in 1910 became a lecturer at his alma mater. During the First World War, Russell was heavily involved in the No-Conscription Fellowship and was fined for writing a leaflet denouncing a sentence of two years in prison for conscientious objectors. He also lost his job at Cambridge. In 1918 he was sentenced to six months in prison for an article he wrote in the *Tribunal*. While in prison, he wrote *Mathematical Philosophy*.

Russell wrote *A History of Western Philosophy* during the Second World War. It was a commercial success and has remained in print since its publication in 1945. The next reading is an extract from Russell's chapter on seventeenth-century philosopher Spinoza, who during his lifetime was considered "a man of appalling wickedness."

Russell was awarded the Nobel Prize in Literature in 1950. He died in 1970 aged ninety-eight after making monumental contributions to logic, philosophy, political theory, religious theory, and history.

Bertrand Russell

from *History of Western Philosophy*

Everything, according to Spinoza, is ruled by an absolute logical necessity. There is no such thing as free will in the mental sphere or chance in the physical world. Everything that happens is a manifestation of God's inscrutable nature, and it is logically impossible that events should be other than they are. This leads to difficulties in regard to sin, which critics were not slow to point out. One of them, observing that, according to Spinoza, everything is decreed by God and is therefore good, asks indignantly: Was it good that Nero should kill his mother? Was it good that Adam ate the apple? Spinoza answers that what was positive in these acts was good, and only what was negative was bad; but negation exists only from the point of view of finite creatures. In God, who alone is completely real, there is no negation, and therefore the evil in what to us seem sins does not exist when they are viewed as parts of the whole. This doctrine, though, in one form or another, it has been held by most mystics, cannot, obviously, be reconciled with the orthodox doctrine of sin and damnation. It is bound up with Spinoza's complete rejection of free will. Although not at all polemical, Spinoza was too honest to conceal his opinions, however shocking to contemporaries; the abhorrence of his teaching is therefore not surprising.

Spinoza regards time as unreal, and therefore all emotions which have to do essentially with an event as future or as past are contrary to reason. "In so far as the mind conceives a thing under the dictate of reason, it is affected equally, whether the idea be of a thing present, past, or future."

This is a hard saying, but it is of the essence of Spinoza's system, and we shall do well to dwell upon it for a moment. In popular estimation, "all's well that ends well"; if the universe is gradually improving, we think better of it than if it is gradually deteriorating, even if the sum of good and evil be the same in the two cases. We are more concerned about a disaster in our own time than in the time of Genghis Khan. According to Spinoza, this is irrational. Whatever happens is part of the eternal timeless world as God sees it; to Him, the date is irrelevant. The wise man, so far as human finitude allows, endeavours to see the world as God sees it, *sub specie æternitatis*, under the aspect of eternity. But, you may retort, we are surely right in being more concerned about future misfortunes, which may possibly be averted, than about past calamities about which we can do nothing. To this argument Spinoza's determinism supplies the answer. Only ignorance makes us think that we can alter the future; what will be will be, and the future is as unalterably fixed as the past. That is why hope and fear are condemned: both depend upon viewing the future as uncertain, and therefore spring from lack of wisdom.

SIMON VAN BOOY

When we acquire, in so far as we can, a vision of the world which is analogous to God's, we see everything as part of the whole, and as necessary to the goodness of the whole. Therefore "the knowledge of evil is an inadequate knowledge." God has no knowledge of evil, because there is no evil to be known; the appearance of evil only arises through regarding parts of the universe as if they were self-subsistent.

Spinoza's outlook is intended to liberate men from the tyranny of fear. "A free man thinks of nothing less than of death; and his wisdom is a meditation not of death, but of life."

In contrasting himself with Spinoza, Leibniz made much of the free will allowed in his system. He had a "principle of sufficient reason," according to which nothing happens without a reason.

One of the most characteristic features of that philosophy is the doctrine of many possible worlds. A world is "possible" if it does not contradict the laws of logic. There are an infinite number of possible worlds, all of which God contemplated before creating the actual world. Being good, God decided to create the best of the possible worlds, and He considered that one to be the best which had the greatest excess of good over evil. He could have created a world containing no evil, but it would not have been so good as the actual world. That is because some great goods are logically bound up with certain evils. To take a trivial illustration, a drink of cold water when you are very thirsty on a hot day may give you such great pleasure that you think the previous thirst, though painful, was worth enduring, because without it the subsequent enjoyment could not have been so great. For theology, it is not such illustrations that are important, but the connection of sin with free will. Free will is a great good, but it was logically impossible for God to bestow free will and at the same time decree that there should be no sin. God therefore decided to make man free, although he foresaw that Adam would eat the apple, and although sin inevitably brought punishment. The world that resulted, although it contains evil, has a greater surplus of good over evil than any other possible world; it is therefore the best of all possible worlds, and the evil that it contains affords no argument against the goodness of God.

This argument apparently satisfied the queen of Prussia. Her serfs continued to suffer the evil, while she continued to enjoy the good, and it was comforting to be assured by a great philosopher that this was just and right.

SIMON VAN BOOY

Caspar David Friedrich was born in 1774 and is known for his unique landscapes with religious themes. Friedrich's early life was traumatic. His mother died when he was seven, and a year after that his sister died. When Friedrich was about thirteen, he watched his younger brother fall through the ice of a frozen lake and drown—apparently trying to save Friedrich himself.

Friedrich is reported to have once said that:

The artist should paint not only what he sees before him, but also what he sees within him. If, however, he sees nothing within him, then he should also refrain from painting that which he sees before him. Otherwise, his pictures will be like those folding screens behind which one expects to find only the sick or the dead.

Although his *Winter Landscape* depicts passionate faith through the lone figure of a praying man whose crutches lay abandoned in the snow, *The Sea of Ice* shows a ship crushed entirely to bits in the Arctic Ocean. This pair of paintings presents an interesting dichotomy between faith and nature.

Caspar David Friedrich, *Winter Landscape*, 1811

Caspar David Friedrich, *The Sea of Ice*, 1823–24

William Shakespeare was born in 1564 in the reign of Queen Elizabeth I. He grew up in Stratford-upon-Avon in central England, one of eight children. Although he probably attended school, he did not go to university. When he was eighteen, he married Anne Hathaway, a woman eight years his senior, who gave birth to their first child about six months after the marriage ceremony. Shakespeare lived most of his adult life in London, where he worked as an actor and playwright with the successful Lord Chamberlain's Men. He died in 1616. His plays have since been translated into every major living language.

William Shakespeare

Hamlet, 5.2., 192–196

Not a whit, we defy augury. There is special providence in the fall of a sparrow. If it be now, 'tis not to come; if it be not to come, it will be now; if it be not now, yet it will come—the readiness is all. Since no man of aught he leaves knows, what is't to leave betimes? Let be.

Colin McGinn was born in England in 1950. In 1972, as a postgraduate student at Oxford, he won the John Locke Prize. Since 1974, Professor McGinn has taught at many of the world's top universities, including University College London, Oxford University, and Rutgers University. He has written dozens of articles in the area of philosophical logic, metaphysics, and the philosophy of language, and around twenty books. He is currently a distinguished professor of philosophy at the University of Miami.

Colin McGinn

from *Shakespeare's Philosophy*

There is no doubt that Hamlet suffers from weakness of will. When the Ghost appears to him for the second time, Hamlet says, "Do you not come your tardy son to chide, That, lapsed in time and passion, lets go by/Th'important acting of your dread command?" and the Ghost speaks in reply of Hamlet's "blunted purpose." Weakness of will has been much discussed by philosophers, because of its puzzling and paradoxical nature. A person judges that he should perform a particular action, and that no contrary consideration counts against the action, and yet he persistently fails to perform it. The intention is there, as clear and strong as anyone could wish, the decision has been made, but no action comes of it. Why? It seems utterly irrational, mysterious, and incomprehensible. Plato even thought that genuine weakness of will is impossible, since no one could fail to act on what they knew they had to do: if you judge that such and such is your moral duty, and there is no fear of untoward consequences, how can you fail to carry out the act? Shouldn't the indicated action follow immediately? Thus Hamlet's inaction strikes us as perplexing. I think Shakespeare is well aware of the puzzle raised by Hamlet's inability to act, but he sees, as a naturalistic observer of human behavior, that weakness of will is not only possible but also quite common. We often, in fact, fail to do what we know we ought to do, even when the action is in our self-interest, and can say little or nothing to explain our failure. Weakness of will is easy; it is explaining it that is hard. What Hamlet primarily needs to perform his act of vengeance is a way to fit it into a dramatic context: it needs to issue from a coherent character playing a part in a drama.

But there is also his melancholy, and his mania—which can seem like two sides of the same coin. Sometimes he seems gloomy and becalmed; at other times he is almost Tourettish in his speech ("I humbly thank you, well, well, well," he ejaculates to Ophelia, and soon blurts out "Ha, ha? Are you honest?"). Montaigne has some interesting remarks in this connection. In "On Sadness" he writes: "The force of extreme sadness inevitably stuns the whole of our soul, impeding her freedom of action. It happens to us when we are suddenly struck with alarm by some piece of really bad news: we are enraptured, seized, paralyzed in all our movements in such a way that, afterwards, when the soul lets herself go with tears and lamentations, she seems to have struggled loose, disentangled herself and become free to range about as she wishes." If we take Hamlet at his word, then the shock and grief he feels at his mother's betrayal, and then his father's murder, work to stun and paralyze him in the way Montaigne suggests. There is no use asking *why* his will becomes paralyzed by such a shock—as if some rational ground could be given for this; it is just a fact of human psychology that this is so. In another passage Montaigne could almost be speaking of Hamlet when he writes:

Is it not true that the soul can be most readily thrown into mania and driven mad by its own quickness, sharpness and nimbleness—in short by the qualities which constitute its strength? Does not the most subtle wisdom produce the most subtle madness? . . . Spirits without number are undermined by their own force and subtlety. There is an Italian poet, fashioned in the atmosphere of the pure poetry of Antiquity, who showed more judgment and genius than any other Italian for many a long year; yet his agile and lively mind has overthrown him; the light has made him blind; his reason's grasp was so precise and so intense that it has left him quite irrational; his quest for knowledge, eager and exacting, has led to his becoming like a dumb beast; his rare aptitude for the activities of the soul has left him with no activity . . . and with no soul. Ought he to be grateful to so murderous a mental agility?

There is no doubting Hamlet's mental agility, his studious nature, his brittle brilliance—but these work to immobilize him and throw him into a state akin to madness. If we combine these two observations of Montaigne's, then we get Hamlet's predicament: a mixture of grief and brilliance leading to confusion and inaction. Hence his famous lines:

I have of late—but wherefore I know not—lost all my mirth, forgone all custom of exercise; and indeed it goes so heavily with my disposition that this goodly frame, the earth, seems to me a sterile promontory. This most excellent canopy of air, look you, this brave o'erhanging, this majestical roof fretted with golden fire—why, it appears no other thing to me than a foul and pestilent congregation of vapours. What a piece of work is man! How noble in reason, how infinite in faculty, in form and moving how express and admirable, in action how like an angel, in apprehension how like a god—the beauty of the world, the paragon of animals! And yet to me what is this quintessence of dust?

On the one hand, he can hymn man and the universe with rare eloquence; on the other, he can avow that it all leaves him cold: his mind can see clearly enough, but his heart isn't in it. What Shakespeare is giving us is a psychological syndrome—a picture of grief, intellectual power, melancholy, and paralysis. This may not fit a Platonic model of the mind as a super-rational agency, always equipped with reasons for action (or inaction), but it is a recognizable psychological profile nonetheless. We must avoid an oversimplified and reductive account of Hamlet's nature, or one that tries to expunge his inherent mystery. As Montaigne says: "Those who strive to account for a man's deeds are never more bewildered than when they try to knit them into one whole and to show them under one light, since they commonly contradict each other in so odd a fashion that it seems impossible that they should all come out of the same shop." It is important that we can recognize the human reality of Hamlet, but that is not the same as trying to make him intelligible, if this means imposing some simplistic or traditional model on his subtleties and shadows.

We are now in a position to examine the most famous speech in the play, and possibly the most famous passage in all literature. "To be, or not to be," it resoundingly begins; not, note, "To live, or not to live." The question employs the most primordial of philosophical concepts, and the most basic metaphysical contrast—that between being and nonbeing. It is stripped down, monosyllabic, and gives the impression of concerning much more than the matter of Hamlet's individual life. It is a question God might ask Himself about whether to create a universe: should there be being or non-being? It is also a question you can imagine someone asking *before* he comes to exist, paradoxically enough: should I come into being or should I not? Is existence worth it? Descartes' *Cogito* is similarly pared down and powerful: "I think, therefore I am"—I have a mind, therefore I have being. Descartes thinks he can prove indubitably that he exists; Hamlet wonders whether this existence is worth a candle. Hamlet is a philosophy student, remember, and he expresses himself with philosophical generality: he finds in his own life a reflection of the most general of questions. Hamlet is confronted by his own being, as every reflective consciousness must be, and hence he can consider its absence. There is no more primal thought: I have being, but my being is contingent. Here is the passage in full:

To be, or not to be; that is the question:
Whether 'tis nobler in the mind to suffer
The slings and arrows of outrageous fortune,
Or to take arms against a sea of troubles,
And, by opposing, end them. To die, to sleep—
No more, and by a sleep to say we end

The heartache and the natural shocks
That flesh is heir to—'tis a consummation
Devoutly to be wished. To die, to sleep.
To sleep, perchance to dream. Ay, there's the rub,
For in that sleep of death what dreams may come
When we have shuffled off this mortal coil
Must give us pause. There's the respect
That makes calamity of so long life,
For who would bear the whips and scorns of time,
Th'oppressor's wrong, the proud man's contumely,
The pangs of disprized love, the law's delay,
The insolence of office, and the spurns
That patient merit of th'unworthy takes,
When he himself might his quietus make
With a bare bodkin? Who would these fardels bear,
To grunt and sweat under a weary life,
But that the dread of something after death,
The undiscovered country from whose bourn,
No traveler returns, puzzles the will,
And makes us rather bear those ills we have
Than fly to others that we know not of?
Thus conscience doth make cowards of us all,
And thus the native hue of resolution
Is sicklied o'er with the pale cast of thought,
And enterprises of great pith and moment

With this regard their currents turn awry,
And lose the name of action.

This passage slides fitfully from one topic to the next, following the mercurial flow of Hamlet's turbulent mind. He quickly interprets his own opening question as about the choice between stoicism and activism (not an obvious interpretation of it, by any means): should he accept his troubles in serenity, or should he act so as to overcome them? This is a question about what sort of person to be, what sort of character to cultivate; and it is notable that Hamlet sees it as a choice, not a piece of fate. But he rapidly moves sideways to the question of whether death is preferable to life. In his melancholic mood he cannot see much advantage in life—his list of life's routine trials and torments is as cogent today as it was then—and his resistance to dying concerns a merely epistemological doubt: how can we know what death is really like? Maybe death is a type of dreaming in which one nightmare succeeds another, so that it is worse than life. Hamlet is expressing a kind of skepticism, to the effect that death might be a lot more disagreeable than we assume—not because of the threat of divine justice but because we have no evidence about what it is really like. Maybe suicide is not the end of a tormented life but the beginning of a new type of torment. We should fear death not because it is the end of something valuable but because it might be a dreadful new beginning. How can we know one way or the other? Descartes worried that our life now might be a dream, but there is an even more unnerving skepticism to contend with once we follow Hamlet's train of thought: that our experience might be just a dream we are having *after death*. How do I really know that I am not *dead* and dreaming? If death is a kind of sleep, it can be accompanied by dreams; but couldn't these dreams simulate ordinary waking life, inviting belief in their illusions? Descartes assumed that we are alive and possibly dreaming in his radical skepticism, but an even more extreme skepticism questions that first assumption: if death and dreaming are compatible, then dream skepticism can extend to the heady possibility that we are all *dead dreamers*. If we were, we would have the same beliefs as we do now, since the appearances would suggest such beliefs; but all these beliefs would be false, including the belief that we are alive. I don't say that Hamlet explicitly raises this extreme brand of skepticism in the quoted passage, but he has the materials with which to raise it—the idea is in the conceptual vicinity. If we add the dream skepticism of *Midsummer Night's Dream* to Hamlet's speculations about a dreaming death, then we reach the radical skeptical possibility of our being under the mistaken impression that we are living, perceiving beings. That is a highly vertiginous thought.

For Hamlet, our ignorance of the nature of death is what deters us from seeking it. It is our consciousness ("conscience") of our ignorance that prevents us opting for death as a way of avoiding the trials of life. This is a very grand form of despair—as if only a fool would not choose death if he could be assured that it was really the end of consciousness! It should be observed how very extreme this despair is, and it is hard to see how Hamlet's actual circumstances can objectively justify it. We could be forgiven for supposing that he is *playing* with despair here—acting the part. For this is the despair of a man who sees nothing positive in life, for whom consciousness itself is an intolerable burden. It is difficult to avoid the impression that his thinking at this point is not altogether sane, that his depressed imagination is running away with him. There is wisdom in his words, to be sure, but there is also madness. We feel sympathy for a man capable of such profound pessimism, but also some puzzlement. We must not forget that Hamlet's voice is not to be identified with Shakespeare's, and that he is certifiably sick in the head. What he offers as wisdom is by no means necessarily what the playwright regards as wisdom: Hamlet is just one character among others, not an infallible oracle (Polonius, despite his confident sententiousness, is full of dubious dicta). This famous speech is as much an expression of Hamlet's derangement as of the truth (according to William Shakespeare) about human life and death. Hamlet is a man troubled by his own thoughts, a victim of them, and his thoughts range into pathological territory at times. When Ophelia interrupts his reverie with "Good my lord, How does your honour for these many a day?" and he replies, "I humbly thank you, well, well, well," we must doubt his assertion of well-being and wonder at the distracted repetition of "well." This is not a man recently engaged upon sober logical reflection, which we as audience are intended to take to the bank, but someone in the grip of paralyzing confusion and grief. Magnificent as the "To be, or not to be" passage is, it must be seen in dramatic context and not excised as if it were Shakespeare's considered judgment on the Meaning of Life. I see it mainly as Hamlet's awareness of his own abyss, his ontological inconstancy, and his propensity to let words get the better of him. Or again, it is Hamlet the student of philosophy toying with possibilities, charting the limits of knowledge, without much regard for common sense or ordinary feeling. This is the man who, when asked what he is reading, dismissively replies "Words, words, words," and is capable of crudely joking to Ophelia of the "No thing" that lies "between maids' legs." He is not a model of discretion and sobriety, and is a master of irony and dissimulation.

"These are wild and whirling words, my lord," Horatio says to him in another connection. We might take a leaf out of Horatio's book when interpreting the "To be" soliloquy.

I shall end this chapter by discussing some incidental lines in *Hamlet* that are philosophically interesting in their own right. One of the most frequently repeated lines in the play is: "There are more things in heaven and earth, Horatio, Than are dreamt of in our philosophy." By "philosophy" here we are to understand the full range of human knowledge, including science. The import of the statement is thus that the universe contains more than we can understand, or even than we can imagine. This is an expression of what philosophers call *realism*—the idea that reality is not limited by the possibilities of human knowledge. Knowledge has its limits, and on the other side of it are things unknown. It is not, then, that reality is determined by what we can know, understand, experience, or conceive; reality, in its intrinsic nature, is quite independent of our epistemological capacities. This is, indeed, the reason that skepticism is a genuine threat: our epistemological faculties can only be inadequate to discovering the world if the world itself is not constituted by those faculties. Knowledge can have limits only because there is something out there that it cannot encompass—facts it cannot reach. We are small creatures in a rich and complex cosmos, and there is no reason to suppose that our "philosophy" can bring everything within its scope, even in principle. Of course, in Shakespeare's time—when knowledge was very restricted—this realist conviction would have sounded a very plausible note to his audience. Hamlet is modestly confessing to the depth of human ignorance.

Joseph Wright of Derby was born in 1734 and concentrated on landscapes, portraits, and science paintings that depict scenes of the British Enlightenment. Educated at Derby Grammar school, Wright taught himself to draw, but then studied with Thomas Hudson, the master of Sir Joshua Reynolds. Wright married in 1773 and had six children, though three died as infants. Joseph Wright's name is associated with Derby as was the custom of that time to distinguish one artist from another with the same name.

Derby's *An Experiment on a Bird in the Air Pump* depicts an early scientific experiment painted in the same way that religious subjects were depicted before the Enlightenment. The children in the background who are distressed by the suffering of the bird may symbolize the harsh, uncompassionate spirit of inquiry associated with the burgeoning art of science.

Joseph Wright of Derby, *An Experiment on a Bird in the Air Pump*, 1768

Albert Camus was born in 1913 to a life of grinding poverty in Algeria. His father died in World War I, and his mother was half-deaf. After suffering a bout of tuberculosis at the age of seventeen, Camus recovered and moved to Paris in 1940, the year before Paris fell under Nazi occupation. Camus, a committed communist, joined the underground Resistance, and he published *L'étranger* (*The Stranger*) in 1942. Camus was always willing to speak out against oppressive elements of government, and wrote not only books, but also plays, which he produced for the theater. Camus is one of the best-known French writers from this postwar period for his works as well as for several famous photographs that give him the glamour of a Hollywood movie star. He died in 1960 in a car accident, three years after receiving the Nobel Prize in Literature. He was survived by his twin children, Catherine and Jean, then age fifteen.

In *The Stranger* (published in Nazi-occupied Paris) the main character, Meursault, behaves in a way that many readers find puzzling. While it may be true that Camus was trying to create a character incapable of telling a lie, many students have associated his behavior with Absurdist and Existentialist views on life. In this particular extract, an incarcerated Meursault wrestles with a prison chaplain, who won't accept Meursault's secular happiness.

Albert Camus

from *The Stranger*

It was at one such moment that I once again refused to see the chaplain. I was lying down, and I could tell from the golden glow in the sky that evening was coming on. I had just denied my appeal and I could feel the steady pulse of my blood circulating inside me. I didn't need to see the chaplain. For the first time in a long time I thought about Marie. The days had been long since she'd stopped writing. That evening I thought about it and told myself that maybe she had gotten tired of being the girlfriend of a condemned man. It also occurred to me that maybe she was sick, or dead. These things happen. How was I to know, since apart from our two bodies, now separated, there wasn't anything to keep us together or even to remind us of each other? Anyway, after that, remembering Marie meant nothing to me. I wasn't interested in her dead. That seemed perfectly normal to me, since I understood very well that people would forget me when I was dead. They wouldn't have anything more to do with me. I wasn't even able to tell myself that it was hard to think those things.

It was at that exact moment that the chaplain came in. When I saw him I felt a little shudder go through me. He noticed it and told me not to be afraid. I told him that it wasn't his usual time. He replied that it was just a friendly visit and had nothing to do with my appeal, which he knew nothing about. He sat down on my bunk and invited me to sit next to him. I refused. All the same, there was something very gentle about him.

He sat there for a few seconds, leaning forward, with his elbows on his knees, looking at his hands.

They were slender and sinewy and they reminded me of two nimble animals. He slowly rubbed one against the other. Then he sat there, leaning forward like that, for so long that for an instant I seemed to forget he was there.

But suddenly he raised his head and looked straight at me. "Why have you refused to see me?" he asked. I said that I didn't believe in God. He wanted to know if I was sure and I said that I didn't see any reason to ask myself that question: it seemed unimportant. He then leaned back against the wall, hands flat on his thighs. Almost as if it wasn't me he was talking to, he remarked that sometimes we think we're sure when in fact we're not. I didn't say anything. He looked at me and asked, "What do you think?" I said it was possible. In any case, I may not have been sure about what really did interest me, but I was absolutely sure about what didn't. And it just so happened that what he was talking about didn't interest me.

He looked away and without moving asked me if I wasn't talking that way out of extreme despair. I explained to him that I wasn't desperate. I was just afraid, which was only natural. "Then God can help you," he said. "Every man I have known in your position has turned to Him." I acknowledged that that was their right. It also meant that they must have had the time for it. As for me, I didn't want anybody's help, and I just didn't have the time to interest myself in what didn't interest me.

At that point he threw up his hands in annoyance but then sat forward and smoothed out the folds of his cassock. When he had finished he started in again, addressing me as "my friend." If he was talking to me this way, it wasn't because I was condemned to die; the way he saw it, we were all condemned to die. But I interrupted him by saying that it wasn't the same thing and that besides, it wouldn't be a consolation anyway. "Certainly," he agreed. "But if you don't die today, you'll die tomorrow, or the next day. And then the same question will arise. How will you face that terrifying ordeal?" I said I would face it exactly as I was facing it now.

At that he stood up and looked me straight in the eye. It was a game I knew well. I played it a lot with Emmanuel and Céleste and usually they were the ones who looked away. The chaplain knew the game well too, I could tell right away: his gaze never faltered. And his voice didn't falter, either, when he said, "Have you no hope at all? And do you really live with the thought that when you die, you die, and nothing remains?" "Yes," I said.

Then he lowered his head and sat back down. He told me that he pitied me. He thought it was more than a man could bear. I didn't feel anything except that he was beginning to annoy me. Then I turned away and went and stood under the skylight. I leaned my shoulder against the wall. Without really following what he was saying, I heard him start asking me questions again. He was talking in an agitated, urgent voice. I could see that he was genuinely upset, so I listened more closely.

He was expressing his certainty that my appeal would be granted, but I was carrying the burden of a sin from which I had to free myself. According to him, human justice was nothing and divine justice was everything. I pointed out that it was the former that had condemned me. His response was that it hadn't washed away my sin for all that. I told him I didn't know what a sin was. All they had told me was that I was guilty. I was guilty, I was paying for it, and nothing more could be asked of me. At that point he stood up again, and the thought occurred to me that in such a narrow cell, if he wanted to move around he didn't have many options. He could either sit down or stand up.

I was staring at the ground. He took a step toward me and stopped, as if he didn't dare come any closer. He looked at the sky through the bars. "You're wrong, my son," he said. "More could be asked of you. And it may be asked." "And what's that?" "You could be asked to see." "See what?"

The priest gazed around my cell and answered in a voice that sounded very weary to me. "Every stone here sweats with suffering, I know that. I have never looked at them without a feeling of anguish. But deep in my heart I know that the most wretched among you have seen a divine face emerge from their darkness. That is the face you are asked to see."

This perked me up a little. I said I had been looking at the stones in these walls for months. There wasn't anything or anyone in the world I knew better. Maybe at one time, way back, I had searched for a face in them. But the face I was looking for was as bright as the sun and the flame of desire—and it belonged to Marie. I had searched for it in vain. Now it was all over. And in any case, I'd never seen anything emerge from any sweating stones.

The chaplain looked at me with a kind of sadness. I now had my back flat against the wall, and light was streaming over my forehead. He muttered a few words I didn't catch and abruptly asked if he could embrace me. "No," I said. He turned and walked over to the wall and slowly ran his hand over it: "Do you really love this earth as much as all that?" he murmured. I didn't answer.

He stood there with his back to me for quite a long time. His presence was grating and oppressive. I was just about to tell him to go, to leave me alone, when all of a sudden, turning toward me, he burst out, "No, I refuse to believe you! I know that at one time or another you've wished for another life." I said of course I had, but it didn't mean any more than wishing to be rich, to be able to swim faster, or to have a more nicely shaped mouth. It was all the same. But he stopped me and wanted to know how I pictured this other life. Then I shouted at him, "One where I could remember this life!" and that's when I told him I'd had enough. He wanted to talk to me about God again, but I went up to him and made one last attempt to explain to him that I had only a little time left and I didn't want to waste it on God. He tried to change the subject by asking me why I was calling him "monsieur" and not "father." That got me mad, and I told him he wasn't my father; he wasn't even on my side.

"Yes, my son," he said, putting his hand on my shoulder, "I am on your side. But you have no way of knowing it, because your heart is blind. I shall pray for you."

Then, I don't know why, but something inside me snapped. I started yelling at the top of my lungs, and I insulted him and told him not to waste his prayers on me. I grabbed him by the collar of his cassock. I was pouring out on him everything that was in my heart, cries of anger and cries of joy. He seemed so certain about everything, didn't he? And yet none of his certainties was worth one hair of a woman's head. He wasn't even sure he was alive, because he was living like a dead man. Whereas it looked as if I was the one who'd come up empty-handed. But I

SIMON VAN BOOY

was sure about me, about everything, surer than he could ever be, sure of my life and sure of the death I had waiting for me. Yes, that was all I had. But at least I had as much of a hold on it as it had on me. I had been right, I was still right, I was always right. I had lived my life one way and I could just as well have lived it another. I had done this and I hadn't done that. I hadn't done this thing but I had done another. And so? It was as if I had waited all this time for this moment and for the first light of this dawn to be vindicated. Nothing, nothing mattered, and I knew why. So did he. Throughout the whole absurd life I'd lived, a dark wind had been rising toward me from somewhere deep in my future, across years that were still to come, and as it passed, this wind leveled whatever was offered to me at the time, in years no more real than the ones I was living. What did other people's deaths or a mother's love matter to me; what did his God or the lives people choose or the fate they think they elect matter to me when we're all elected by the same fate, me and billions of privileged people like him who also called themselves my brothers? Couldn't he see, couldn't he see that? Everybody was privileged. There were only privileged people. The others would all be condemned one day. And he would be condemned, too. What would it matter if he were accused of murder and then executed because he didn't cry at his mother's funeral? Salamano's dog was worth just as much as his wife. The little robot woman was just as guilty as the Parisian woman Masson married, or as Marie, who had wanted me to marry her. What did it matter that Raymond was as much my friend as Céleste, who was worth a lot more than him? What did it matter that Marie now offered her lips to a new Meursault? Couldn't he, couldn't this condemned man see . . . And that from somewhere deep in my future . . . All the shouting had me gasping for air. But they were already tearing the chaplain from my grip and the guards were threatening me. He calmed them, though, and looked at me for a moment without saying anything. His eyes were full of tears. Then he turned and disappeared.

With him gone, I was able to calm down again. I was exhausted and threw myself on my bunk. I must have fallen asleep, because I woke up with the stars in my face. Sounds of the countryside were drifting in. Smells of night, earth, and salt air were cooling my temples. The wondrous peace of that sleeping summer flowed through me like a tide. Then, in the dark hour before dawn, sirens blasted. They were announcing departures for a world that now and forever meant nothing to me. For the first time in a long time I thought about Maman. I felt as if I understood why at the end of her life she had taken a "fiancé," why she had played at beginning again. Even there, in that home where lives were fading out, evening was a kind

SIMON VAN BOOY

of wistful respite. So close to death, Maman must have felt free then and ready to live it all again. Nobody, nobody had the right to cry over her. And I felt ready to live it all again too. As if that blind rage had washed me clean, rid me of hope; for the first time, in that night alive with signs and stars, I opened myself to the gentle indifference of the world. Finding it so much like myself—so like a brother, really—I felt that I had been happy and that I was happy again. For everything to be consummated, for me to feel less alone, I had only to wish that there be a large crowd of spectators the day of my execution and that they greet me with cries of hate.

Born in 1891, Henry Miller was a groundbreaking American novelist whose writing blended humor, philosophical rhetoric, sexual exploration, and autobiography. During his somewhat Bohemian life, Miller had an intimate friendship with Anaïs Nin (who paid for the first printing of *Tropic of Cancer*). Two of his most famous books are *Tropic of Cancer* (1934) and *Tropic of Capricorn* (1938). Both books were banned in the United States until 1961. *Tropic of Capricorn*, the sequel to *Tropic of Cancer*, follows Miller's life in New York in the 1920s, chronicling his development as a writer and describing outrageous sexual exploits. Miller married five times and died in 1980 in Southern California at age eighty-nine.

Henry Miller

from *Tropic of Capricorn*

Once you have given up the ghost, everything follows with dead certainty, even in the midst of chaos. From the beginning it was never anything but chaos: it was a fluid which enveloped me, which I breathed in through the gills. In the substrata, where the moon shone steady and opaque, it was smooth and fecundating; above it was a jangle and a discord. In everything I quickly saw the opposite, the contradiction, and between the real and the unreal the irony, the paradox. I was my own worst enemy. There was nothing I wished to do which I could just as well not do. Even as a child, when I lacked for nothing, I wanted to die: I wanted to surrender because I saw no sense in struggling. I felt that nothing would be proved, substantiated, added or subtracted by continuing an existence which I had not asked for. Everybody around me was a failure, or if not a failure, ridiculous. Especially the successful ones. The successful ones bored me to tears. I was sympathetic to a fault, but it was not sympathy that made me so. It was a purely negative quality, a weakness which blossomed at the mere sight of human misery. I never helped any one expecting that it would do any good; I helped because I was helpless to do otherwise. To want to change the condition of affairs seemed futile to me; nothing would be altered, I was convinced, except by a change of heart, and who could change the hearts of men? Now and then a friend was converted: it was something to make me puke. I had no more need of God than He had of me, and if there were one, I often said to myself, I would meet Him calmly and spit in His face.

SIMON VAN BOOY

ESTRAGON

[GIVING UP AGAIN] Nothing to be done.

VLADIMIR

[ADVANCING WITH SHORT, STIFF STRIDES, LEGS WIDE APART]
I'm beginning to come round to that opinion.

—*Samuel Beckett from the first two lines*
of Waiting for Godot

VLADIMIR

Well? Shall we go?

ESTRAGON

Yes, let's go.

{THEY DO NOT MOVE.}

—*Samuel Beckett from the last two lines*
of Waiting for Godot

Jean-Paul Sartre, born in 1905, was a contemporary and friend of Albert Camus. He was also the leading figure of Parisian Existentialism and wrote plays and novels, in addition to being a philosopher. Sartre was the first Nobel Prize recipient in history to refuse the prize when it was awarded to him in 1964. He died in 1980. His funeral attracted twenty thousand mourners.

In 1945 Sartre outlined his ideas in the famous lecture "Existentialism and Humanism," which in 1946 became a book of the same name and defined the key points of Existentialism.

Jean-Paul Sartre

from "Existentialism and Humanism"

Atheistic existentialism, of which I am a representative, declares with greater consistency that if God does not exist there is at least one being whose existence comes before its essence, a being which exists before it can be defined by any conception of it. That being is man or, as Heidegger has it, the human reality. What do we mean by saying that existence precedes essence? We mean that man first of all exists, encounters himself, surges up in the world—and defines himself afterwards. If man as the existentialist sees him is not definable, it is because to begin with he is nothing. He will not be anything until later, and then he will be what he makes of himself. Thus, there is no human nature, because there is no God to have a conception of it. Man simply is.

To choose between this or that is at the same time to affirm the value of that which is chosen; for we are unable ever to choose the worse. What we choose is always the better; and nothing can be better for us unless it is better for all.

For if indeed existence precedes essence, one will never be able to explain one's action by reference to a given and specific human nature; in other words, there is no determinism—man is free, man *is* freedom. Nor, on the other hand, if God does not exist, are we provided with any values or commands that could legitimise our behaviour. Thus we have neither behind us, nor before us in a luminous realm of values, any means of justification or excuse. We are left alone, without excuse. That is what I mean when I say that man is condemned to be free. Condemned, because he did not create himself, yet is nevertheless at liberty, and from the moment that he is thrown into this world he is responsible for everything he does. The existentialist does not believe in the power of passion.

As an example by which you may the better understand this state of abandonment, I will refer to the case of a pupil of mine, who sought me out in the following circumstances. His father was quarrelling with his mother and was also inclined to be a "collaborator"; his elder brother had been killed in the German offensive of 1940 and this young man, with a sentiment somewhat primitive but generous, burned to avenge him. His mother was living alone with him, deeply afflicted by the semi-treason of his father and by the death of her eldest son, and her one consolation was in this young man. But he, at this moment, had the choice between going to England to join the Free French Forces or of staying near his mother and helping her to live. He fully realised that this woman lived only for him and that his disappearance—or perhaps his death— would plunge her into despair. He also realised that, concretely and in fact, every action he performed on his mother's behalf would be sure of effect in the sense of aiding her to live, where as anything he did in order to go and fight would be an ambiguous action which might vanish like water into sand and serve no purpose. For instance, to set out for England he would have to wait indefinitely in a Spanish camp on the way through Spain; or, on arriving in England or in Algiers he might be put into an office to fill up forms. Consequently, he found himself confronted by two very different modes of action; the one concrete, immediate, but directed towards only one individual; and the other an action addressed to an end infinitely greater, a national collectivity, but for that very reason ambiguous—and it might be frustrated on the way. At the same time, he was hesitating between two kinds of morality; on the one side the morality of sympathy, of personal devotion and, on the other side, a morality of wider scope but of more debatable validity. He had to choose between those two. What could help him to choose? Could the Christian doctrine? No. Christian doctrine says: Act with charity, love your neighbour, deny yourself for others, choose the way which is hardest, and so forth. But which is the harder road? To whom does one owe the more brotherly love, the patriot or the mother? Which is the more useful aim, the general one of fighting in and for the whole community, or the precise aim of helping one particular person to live? Who can give an answer to that *à priori*? No one. Nor is it given in any ethical scripture. The Kantian ethic says, Never regard another as a means, but always as an end.

Very well; if I remain with my mother, I shall be regarding her as the end and not as a means: but by the same token I am in danger of treating as means those who are fighting on my behalf; and the converse is also true, that if I go to the aid of the combatants I shall be treating them as the end at the risk of treating my mother as a means.

If values are uncertain, if they are still too abstract to determine the particular, concrete case under consideration, nothing remains but to trust in our instincts. That is what this young man tried to do; and when I saw him he said, "In the end, it is feeling that counts; the direction in which it is really pushing me is the one I ought to choose. If I feel that I love my mother enough to sacrifice everything else for her—my will to be avenged, all my longings for action and adventure—then I stay with her. If, on the contrary, I feel that my love for her is not enough, I go." But how does one estimate the strength of a feeling? The value of his feeling for his mother was determined precisely by the fact that he was standing by her. I may say that I love a certain friend enough to sacrifice such or such a sum of money for him, but I cannot prove that unless I have done it. I may say, "I love my mother enough to remain with her," if actually I have remained with her. I can only estimate the strength of this affection if I have performed an action by which it is defined and ratified. But if I then appeal to this affection to justify my action, I find myself drawn into a vicious circle.

SIMON VAN BOOY

Moreover, as Gide has very well said, a sentiment which is play-acting and one which is vital are two things that are hardly distinguishable one from another. To decide that I love my mother by staying beside her, and to play a comedy the upshot of which is that I do so—these are nearly the same thing. In other words, feeling is formed by the deeds that one does; therefore I cannot consult it as a guide to action. And that is to say that I can neither seek within myself for an authentic impulse to action, nor can I expect, from some ethic, formulae that will enable me to act. You may say that the youth did, at least, go to a professor to ask for advice. But if you seek counsel—from a priest, for example—you have selected that priest; and at bottom you already knew, more or less, what he would advise. In other words, to choose an adviser is nevertheless to commit oneself by that choice. If you are a Christian, you will say, Consult a priest; but there are collaborationists, priests who are resisters and priests who wait for the tide to turn; which will you choose? Had this young man chosen a priest of the resistance, or one of the collaboration, he would have decided beforehand the kind of advice he was to receive. Similarly, in coming to me, he knew what advice I should give him, and I had but one reply to make. You are free, therefore choose—that is to say, invent. No rule of general morality can show you what you ought to do: no signs are vouch-safed in this world.

Plato was born c. 428 BCE, and lived until c. 348 BCE. He is one of the greatest known Western philosophers, and the most famous student of Socrates. Plato's books consist of dialogues between his great teacher Socrates and others. His most popular dialogues include *Symposium*, *Republic*, *Phaedrus*, and *Phaedo*—the latter of which contains a vivid account of Socrates's final hours. Plato's influence on philosophy is staggering, for not only did he explore the ideas of his teacher, Socrates, but he was also Aristotle's teacher.

In Plato's famous *Allegory of the Cave*, he suggests that people spend their lives chained up in a cave, mistaking shadows on the walls for real objects. Therefore, anything they think they know is based on a misperception of objective reality, which means that their decisions are based on false perceptions.

Plato

Allegory of the Cave

And now, I said, let me show in a figure how far our nature is enlightened or unenlightened:—Behold! human beings living in an underground den, which has a mouth open towards the light and reaching all along the den; here they have been from their childhood, and have their legs and necks chained so that they cannot move, and can only see before them, being prevented by the chains from turning round their heads. Above and behind them a fire is blazing at a distance, and between the fire and the prisoners there is a raised way; and you will see, if you look, a low wall built along the way, like the screen which marionette players have in front of them, over which they show the puppets.

I see.

And do you see, I said, men passing along the wall carrying all sorts of vessels, and statues and figures of animals made of wood and stone and various materials, which appear over the wall? Some of them are talking, others silent.

You have shown me a strange image, and they are strange prisoners.

Like ourselves, I replied; and they see only their own shadows, or the shadows of one another, which the fire throws on the opposite wall of the cave?

True, he said; how could they see anything but the shadows if they were never allowed to move their heads?

And of the objects which are being carried in like manner they would only see the shadows?

Yes, he said.

And if they were able to converse with one another, would they not suppose that they were naming what was actually before them?

Very true.

And suppose further that the prison had an echo which came from the other side, would they not be sure to fancy when one of the passers-by spoke that the voice which they heard came from the passing shadow?

No question, he replied.

To them, I said, the truth would be literally nothing but the shadows of the images.

That is certain.

And now look again, and see what will naturally follow if the prisoners are released and disabused of their error. At first, when any of them is liberated and compelled suddenly to stand up and turn his neck round and walk and look towards the light, he will suffer sharp pains; the glare will distress him, and he will be unable to see the realities of which in his former state he had seen the shadows; and then conceive some one saying to him, that what he saw before was an illusion, but that now, when he is approaching nearer to being and his eye is turned towards more real existence, he has a clearer vision,—what will be his reply? And you may further imagine that his instructor is pointing to the objects as they pass and requiring him to name them,—will he not be perplexed? Will he not fancy that the shadows which he formerly saw are truer than the objects which are now shown to him?

Far truer.

And if he is compelled to look straight at the light, will he not have a pain in his eyes which will make him turn away to take refuge in the objects of vision which he can see, and which he will conceive to be in reality clearer than the things which are now being shown to him?

True, he said.

And suppose once more, that he is reluctantly dragged up a steep and rugged ascent, and held fast until he is forced into the presence of the sun himself, is he not likely to be pained and irritated? When he approaches the light his eyes will be dazzled, and he will not be able to see anything at all of what are now called realities.

Not all in a moment, he said.

He will require to grow accustomed to the sight of the upper world. And first he will see the shadows best, next the reflections of men and other objects in the water, and then the objects themselves; then he will gaze upon the light of the moon and the stars and the spangled heaven; and he will see the sky and the stars by night better than the sun or the light of the sun by day?

Certainly.

Last of all he will be able to see the sun, and not mere reflections of him in the water, but he will see him in his own proper place, and not in another; and he will contemplate him as he is.

Certainly.

He will then proceed to argue that this is he who gives the season and the years, and is the guardian of all that is in the visible world, and in a certain way the cause of all things which he and his fellows have been accustomed to behold?

Clearly, he said, he would first see the sun and then reason about him.

And when he remembered his old habitation, and the wisdom of the den and his fellow-prisoners, do you not suppose that he would felicitate himself on the change, and pity them?

Certainly, he would.

And if they were in the habit of conferring honours among themselves on those who were quickest to observe the passing shadows and to remark which of them went before, and which followed after, and which were together, and who were therefore best able to draw conclusions as to the future, do you think that he would care for such honours and glories, or envy the possessors of them? Would he not say with Homer,

"Better to be the poor servant of a poor master,"

and to endure anything, rather than think as they do and live after their manner?

Yes, he said, I think that he would rather suffer anything than entertain these false notions and live in this miserable manner.

Imagine once more, I said, such a one coming suddenly out of the sun to be replaced in his old situation; would he not be certain to have his eyes full of darkness?

To be sure, he said.

And if there were a contest, and he had to compete in measuring the shadows with the prisoners who had never moved out of the den, while his sight was still weak, and before his eyes had become steady (and the time which would be needed to acquire this new habit of sight might be very considerable), would he not be ridiculous? Men would say of him that up he went and down he came without his eyes; and that it was better not even to think of ascending; and if any one tried to loose another and lead him up to the light, let them only catch the offender, and they would put him to death.

No question, he said.

This entire allegory, I said, you may now append, dear Glaucon, to the previous argument; the prison-house is the world of sight, the light of the fire is the sun, and you will not misapprehend me if you interpret the journey upwards to be the ascent of the soul into the intellectual world according to my poor belief, which, at your desire, I have expressed—whether rightly or wrongly God knows. But, whether true or false, my opinion is that in the world of knowledge the idea of good appears last of all, and is seen only with an effort; and, when seen, is also inferred to be the universal author of all things beautiful and right, parent of light and of the lord of light in this visible world, and the immediate source of reason and truth in the intellectual; and that this is the power upon which he who would act rationally either in public or private life must have his eye fixed.

I agree, he said, as far as I am able to understand you.

Moreover, I said, you must not wonder that those who attain to this beatific vision are unwilling to descend to human affairs; for their souls are ever hastening into the upper world where they desire to dwell; which desire of theirs is very natural, if our allegory may be trusted.

Yes, very natural.

And is there anything surprising in one who passes from divine contemplations to the evil state of man, misbehaving himself in a ridiculous manner; if, while his eyes are blinking and before he has become accustomed to the surrounding darkness, he is compelled to fight in courts of law, or in other places, about the images or the shadows of images of justice, and is endeavouring to meet the conceptions of those who have never yet seen absolute justice?

Anything but surprising, he replied.

Any one who has common sense will remember that the bewilderments of the eyes are of two kinds, and arise from two causes, either from coming out of the light or from going into the light, which is true of the mind's eye, quite as much as of the bodily eye; and he who remembers this when he sees any one whose vision is perplexed and weak, will not be too ready to laugh; he will first ask whether that soul of man has come out of the brighter life, and is unable to see because unaccustomed to the dark, or having turned from darkness to the day is dazzled by excess of light. And he will count the one happy in his condition and state of being, and he will pity the other; or, if he have a mind to laugh at the soul which comes from below into the light, there will be more reason in this than in the laugh which greets him who returns from above out of the light into the den.

That, he said, is a very just distinction.

But then, if I am right, certain professors of education must be wrong when they say that they can put a knowledge into the soul which was not there before, like sight into blind eyes.

They undoubtedly say this, he replied.

Whereas, our argument shows that the power and capacity of learning exists in the soul already; and that just as the eye was unable to turn from darkness to light without the whole body, so too the instrument of knowledge can only by the movement of the whole soul be turned from the world of becoming into that of being, and learn by degrees to endure the sight of being, and of the brightest and best of being, or in other words, of the good.

Very true.

Janet Frame was born in New Zealand in 1924, to a railroad engineer and a maid. As a girl, she experienced the death of two sisters by drowning, and later as a young trainee teacher, she suffered a nervous breakdown after an inspector stepped into the classroom. This breakdown led to an eight-year stretch in a mental hospital, where Frame was misdiagnosed with schizophrenia. During her institutionalization, Frame received about two hundred electroshock treatments, and narrowly avoided a lobotomy after a member of the hospital staff read that she had been awarded a top literary prize. After her emancipation, Frame traveled widely, often to the United States, where she developed friendships with important American writers and artists like Theophilus Brown, May Sarton, and Barbara Wersba. In the 1980s, Frame's three-volume autobiography thrust her into the spotlight when director Jane Campion adapted the trilogy for film. *An Angel at My Table* was released in 1990 and introduced Frame to a new generation of readers. Janet Frame died in 2004 after writing over twenty books.

In her novel *The Carpathians*, Frame further explores the Platonic idea that questions our perceptions. If we are in fact not perceiving reality as it really is—then do our decisions not matter because we've essentially become misinformed?

Janet Frame

from *The Carpathians*

"I expect you'll get to know us in Kowhai Street."

"The kowhais are the trees, I guess," Mattina said.

"Yes, New Zealand trees. And there's native bush along the east of Gillespie Street, towards the mountains. You'll likely see it in your stay here . . . two months, is it?"

"Two months."

"You'll certainly get to know everyone here. And our street has a neighbourhood watch scheme where you look out for the others in the street, report anything suspicious day or night . . . it works, too."

"I'm sure it does," Mattina said, feeling increasingly bored and tired. "Has Puamahara so much crime?"

"You'd be surprised. Everything has changed. Burglary, rape, murder. . . ."

Mattina frowned with disbelief.

"It's true. Oh, and would you like some carnations for your house? I get the rejects but the rejects are often better than the others. Flaws in the blossom, a slight imperfection of colour, a misshapen petal, features you wouldn't normally notice."

"I'd love some flowers," Mattina said.

"I'll leave them on your doorstep if you're out."

"Of course."

Mattina thought as she entered the house that she and Dorothy Townsend were not unlike in appearance: both were small and dark, but where Dorothy's cheeks were rosy, her skin fair, Mattina's skin was sallow beneath her suntan. Dorothy was much younger. Mattina felt she had seldom spent so much time paying attention to trees and flowers. She couldn't remember when last she had given them any thought. What else can I expect, she said to herself, in the town of the Memory Flower? And now I have been offered as much as I want of rejected carnations, and perhaps never know why they have been rejected. Who knows, she thought, feeling tiredness overcome her and rebelling against a stupid confusion in her mind, we could all be rejects in a rejected world and never know or dream that simultaneously the chosen flourish elsewhere in a perfect world.

SIMON VAN BOOY

Fernando António Nogueira Pessoa was born in Lisbon in 1888. When he was seven, his family moved to Durban, a British colony in South Africa. He returned to Lisbon in 1905 and never left until his death thirty years later. He is famous for using heteronyms, where he would write under different personalities with different writing styles. Although he established about seventy heteronyms, his main voices were Alberto Caeiro, Ricardo Reis, and Alvaro de Campos. He earned a living as a commercial translator and wanted to live in the simplest way possible—though he is reported to have always been elegantly dressed. When he died, approximately twenty-five thousand papers, fragments, and notes were discovered in his trunk, most of which were unpublished.

Alberto Caeiro

"Poem XXVIII" from *The Keeper of Sheep*

I read today almost two pages
In a book by a mystic poet,
And laughed like one who has cried a lot.

Mystic poets are sick philosophers,
And philosophers are madmen.

Because mystic poets say that flowers feel
And say that stones have a soul
And that rivers have ecstasies in moonlight.

But flowers, if they felt at all, wouldn't be flowers,
They'd be people;
And if stones had a soul, they'd be living things, not stones;
And if rivers had ecstasies in moonlight,
They'd be sick men.

It would take not to know what flowers and stones and
    rivers are
To talk about their feelings.
To talk about the soul of stones, flowers, and rivers
Is to talk about oneself and one's own false thoughts.

Thank God that stones are only stones,

And that rivers are nothing but rivers,

And that flowers are just flowers.

As for myself, I write the prose of my verses

And I am satisfied.

Because I know that I understand Nature from the outside;

And I don't understand it from the inside

Because Nature has no inside;

Otherwise it wouldn't be Nature.

—Translated from the Portuguese by Patricio Ferrari

Ludwig Wittgenstein was born in 1889 in Austria, to a prominent Viennese family. Although Wittgenstein's family was very wealthy, they suffered from numerous psychological disorders, and it is reported that three of Wittgenstein's brothers committed suicide. When his father died, young Wittgenstein inherited a hefty amount of money but gave most of it away, choosing to live in an unfurnished apartment while at Cambridge University where he studied with Bertrand Russell, his great friend and mentor. He is also reputed to have suffered from terrible bouts of fury, which bordered on madness. He died of cancer in 1951. Wittgenstein is perhaps most regarded for his exploration into the relationships between the world, thought, and language.

Wittgenstein's famous *Tractatus Logico-Philosophicus* explores his view that the problems of philosophy are braided with misunderstandings about language, and so our task should be to study the nature and logic of language. In this first book, Wittgenstein wanted to explain the complex workings of language—for it was his belief that what we can say is the same as what we can think. Therefore, by understanding the complexities of language and its relationship to the world, one would understand the boundaries of what can be said and what can be thought. For Wittgenstein, trying to talk about anything ("mystical") beyond those boundaries was the same as trying to say what cannot be said and think what cannot be thought—though not because of deficiencies within the problems themselves, but due to the limits of language.

Ludwig Wittgenstein

from *Tractatus Logico-Philosophicus*

This book will perhaps only be understood by those who have themselves already thought the thoughts which are expressed in it—or similar thoughts. It is therefore not a textbook. Its object would be attained if there were one person who read it with understanding and to whom it afforded pleasure.

The book deals with the problems of philosophy and shows, as I believe, that the method of formulating these problems rests on the misunderstanding of the logic of our language. Its whole meaning could be summed up somewhat as follows: What can be said at all can be said clearly; and whereof one cannot speak thereof one must be silent.

The book will, therefore, draw a limit to thinking, or rather—not to thinking, but to the expression of thoughts; for in order to draw a limit to thinking we should have to be able to think both sides of this limit (we should therefore have to be able to think what cannot be thought).

The limit can, therefore, only be drawn in language and what lies on the other side of the limit will be simply nonsense.

How far my efforts agree with those of other philosophers I will not decide. Indeed what I have here written makes no claim to novelty in points of detail; and therefore

I give no sources, because it is indifferent to me whether what I have thought has already been thought before me by another.

I will only mention that to the great works of Frege and the writings of my friend Bertrand Russell I owe in large measure the stimulation of my thoughts.

If this work has a value it consists in two things. First that in it thoughts are expressed, and this value will be the greater the better the thoughts are expressed. The more the nail has been hit on the head.—Here I am conscious that I have fallen far short of the possible. Simply because my powers are insufficient to cope with the task.—May others come and do it better.

On the other hand the *truth* of the thoughts communicated here seems to me unassailable and definitive. I am, therefore, of the opinion that the problems have in essentials been finally solved. And if I am not mistaken in this, then the value of this work secondly consists in the fact that it shows how little has been done when these problems have been solved.

LUDWIG WITTGENSTEIN
Vienna, 1918

TRACTATUS LOGICO-PHILOSOPHICUS

1*   The world is everything that is the case.

1.1   The world is the totality of facts, not of things.

1.11   The world is determined by the facts, and by these being *all* the facts.

1.12   For the totality of facts determines both what is the case, and also all that is not the case.

1.13   The facts in logical space are the world.

1.2   The world divides into facts.

1.21   Anyone can either be the case or not be the case, and everything else remain the same.

2   What is the case, the fact, is the existence of atomic facts.

2.01   An atomic fact is a combination of objects (entities, things).

2.011   It is essential to a thing that it can be a constituent part of an atomic fact.

2.012   In logic nothing is accidental: if a thing *can* occur

---

* The decimal figures as numbers of the separate propositions indicate the logical importance of the propositions, the emphasis laid upon them in my exposition. The propositions *n*.1, *n*.2, *n*.3, etc., are comments on proposition No. *n*; the propositions *n.m*1, *n.m*2, etc., are comments on the proposition No. *n.m*; and so on.

SIMON VAN BOOY

in an atomic fact the possibility of that atomic fact must already be prejudged in the thing.

2.0121   It would, so to speak, appear as an accident, when to a thing that could exist alone on its own account, subsequently a state of affairs could be made to fit.

If things can occur in atomic facts, this possibility must already lie in them.

(A logical entity cannot be merely possible. Logic treats of every possibility, and all possibilities are its facts.)

Just as we cannot think of spatial objects at all apart from space, or temporal objects apart from time, so we cannot think of *any* object apart from the possibility of its connexion with other things.

If I can think of an object in the context of an atomic fact, I cannot think of it apart from the *possibility* of this context.

2.0122   The thing is independent, in so far as it can occur in all *possible* circumstances, but this form of independence is a form of connexion with the atomic fact, a form of dependence. (It is impossible for words to occur in two different ways, alone and in the proposition.)

2.0123   If I know an object, then I also know all the possibilities of its occurrence in atomic facts.

Every such possibility must lie in the nature of the object.)

A new possibility cannot subsequently be found.

2.01231 In order to know an object, I must know not its external but all its internal qualities.

2.0124 If all objects are given, then thereby are all *possible* atomic facts also given.

2.013 Everything is, as it were, in a space of possible atomic facts. I can think of this space as empty, but not of the thing without the space.

2.0131 A spatial object must lie in infinite space. (A point in space is a place for an argument.)

A speck in a visual field need not be red, but it must have a colour; it has, so to speak, a colour space round it. A tone must have a pitch, the object of the sense of touch a hardness, etc.

2.014 Objects contain the possibility of all states of affairs.

2.0141 The possibility of its occurrence in atomic facts is the form of the object.

2.02 The object is simple.

2.0201 Every statement about complexes can be analysed into a statement about their constituent parts, and into those propositions which completely describe the complexes.

2.021   Objects form the substance of the world. Therefore they cannot be compound.

2.0211   If the world had no substance, then whether a proposition had sense would depend on whether another proposition was true.

2.0212   It would then be impossible to form a picture of the world (true or false).

2.022   It is clear that however different from the real one an imagined world may be, it must have something—a form—in common with the real world.

2.023   This fixed form consists of the objects.

2.0231   The substance of the world *can* only determine a form and not any material properties. For these are first presented by the propositions—first formed by the configuration of the objects.

2.0232   Roughly speaking: objects are colourless.

2.0233   Two objects of the same logical form are—apart from their external properties—only differentiated from one another in that they are different.

2.02331 Either a thing has properties which no other has, and then one can distinguish it straight away from the others by a description and refer to it; or, on the other hand, there are several things which have the totality of their properties in common, and then it is quite impossible to point to any one of them.

For if a thing is not distinguished by anything, I cannot distinguish it—for otherwise it would be distinguished.

2.024   Substance is what exists independently of what is the case.

2.025   It is form and content.

2.0251 Space, time and colour (colouredness) are forms of objects.

2.026   Only if there are objects can there be a fixed form of the world.

2.027   The fixed, the existent and the object are one.

2.0271 The object is the fixed, the existent; the configuration is the changing, the variable.

2.0272 The configuration of the objects forms the atomic fact.

2.03   In the atomic fact objects hang one in another, like the members of a chain.

2.031   In the atomic fact the objects are combined in a definite way.

2.032   The way in which objects hang together in the atomic fact is the structure of the atomic fact.

2.033   The form is the possibility of the structure.

2.034   The structure of the fact consists of the structures of the atomic facts.

2.04   The totality of existent atomic facts is the world.

2.05   The totality of existent atomic facts also determines which atomic facts do not exist.

2.06   The existence and nonexistence of atomic facts is the reality.

        (The existence of atomic facts we also call a positive fact, their nonexistence a negative fact.)

2.061   Atomic facts are independent of one another.

2.062   From the existence or nonexistence of an atomic fact we cannot infer the existence or nonexistence of another.

2.063   The total reality is the world.

2.1   We make to ourselves pictures of facts.

2.11   The picture presents the facts in logical space, the existence and nonexistence of atomic facts.

2.12   The picture is a model of reality.

2.13   To the objects correspond in the picture the elements of the picture.

2.131   The elements of the picture stand, in the picture, for the objects.

2.14   The picture consists in the fact that its elements are combined with one another in a definite way.

2.141   The picture is a fact.

2.15   That the elements of the picture are combined with one another in a definite way, represents that the things are so combined with one another.

This connexion of the elements of the picture is called its structure, and the possibility of this structure is called the form of representation of the picture.

2.151 The form of representation is the possibility that the things are combined with one another as are the elements of the picture.

2.1511 Thus the picture is linked with reality; it reaches up to it.

2.1512 It is like a scale applied to reality.

2.15121 Only the outermost points of the dividing lines *touch* the object to be measured.

2.1513 According to this view the representing relation which makes it a picture, also belongs to the picture.

2.1514 The representing relation consists of the coordinations of the elements of the picture and the things.

2.1515 These coordinations are as it were the feelers of its elements with which the picture touches reality.

2.16 In order to be a picture a fact must have something in common with what it pictures.

2.161 In the picture and the pictured there must be something identical in order that the one can be a picture of the other at all.

2.17 What the picture must have in common with reality

in order to be able to represent it after its manner—rightly or falsely—is its form of representation.

2.171   The picture can represent every reality whose form it has.

The spatial picture, everything spatial, the coloured, everything coloured, etc.

2.172   The picture, however, cannot represent its form of representation; it shows it forth.

2.173   The picture represents its object from without (its standpoint is its form of representation), therefore the picture represents its object rightly or falsely.

2.174   But the picture cannot place itself outside of its form of representation.

2.18   What every picture, of whatever form, must have in common with reality in order to be able to represent it at all—rightly or falsely—is the logical form, that is, the form of reality.

2.181   If the form of representation is the logical form, then the picture is called a logical picture.

2.182   Every picture is *also* a logical picture. (On the other hand, for example, not every picture is spatial.)

2.19   The logical picture can depict the world.

2.2   The picture has the logical form of representation in common with what it pictures.

2.201   The picture depicts reality by representing a possibility of the existence and nonexistence of atomic facts.

2.202   The picture represents a possible state of affairs in logical space.

2.203   The picture contains the possibility of the state of affairs which it represents.

2.21   The picture agrees with reality or not; it is right or wrong, true or false.

2.22   The picture represents what it represents, independently of its truth or falsehood, through the form of representation.

2.221   What the picture represents is its sense.

2.222   In the agreement or disagreement of its sense with reality, its truth or falsity consists.

2.223   In order to discover whether the picture is true or false we must compare it with reality.

2.224   It cannot be discovered from the picture alone whether it is true or false.

2.225   There is no picture which is a priori true.

3   The logical picture of the facts is the thought.

3.001   "An atomic fact is thinkable"—means: we can imagine it.

3.01   The totality of true thoughts is a picture of the world.

3.02   The thought contains the possibility of the state of affairs which it thinks.

          What is thinkable is also possible.

3.03   We cannot think anything unlogical, for otherwise we should have to think unlogically.

3.031   It used to be said that God could create everything, except what was contrary to the laws of logic. The truth is, we could not *say* of an "unlogical" world how it would look.

3.032   To present in language anything which "contradicts logic" is as impossible as in geometry to present by its coordinates a figure which contradicts the laws of space; or to give the coordinates of a point which does not exist.

3.0321   We could present spatially an atomic fact which contradicted the laws of physics, but not one which contradicted the laws of geometry.

3.04   An a priori true thought would be one whose possibility guaranteed its truth.

3.05   We could only know a priori that a thought is true if its truth was to be recognized from the thought itself (without an object of comparison).

3.1   In the proposition the thought is expressed perceptibly through the senses.

3.11   We use the sensibly perceptible sign (sound or

written sign, etc.) of the proposition as a projection of the possible state of affairs.

The method of projection is the thinking of the sense of the proposition.

3.12 The sign through which we express the thought I call the propositional sign. And the proposition is the propositional sign in its projective relation to the world.

3.13 To the proposition belongs everything which belongs to the projection; but not what is projected.

Therefore the possibility of what is projected but not this itself.

In the proposition, therefore, its sense is not yet contained, but the possibility of expressing it.

("The content of the proposition" means the content of the significant proposition.)

In the proposition the form of its sense is contained, but not its content.

3.14 The propositional sign consists in the fact that its elements, the words, are combined in it in a definite way.

The propositional sign is a fact.

3.141 The proposition is not a mixture of words (just as the musical theme is not a mixture of tones).

The proposition is articulate.

3.142   Only facts can express a sense, a class of names cannot.

3.143   That the propositional sign is a fact is concealed by the ordinary form of expression, written or printed.

(For in the printed proposition, for example, the sign of a proposition does not appear essentially different from a word. Thus it was possible for Frege to call the proposition a compounded name.)

3.1431   The essential nature of the propositional sign becomes very clear when we imagine it made up of spatial objects (such as tables, chairs, books) instead of written signs.

The mutual spatial position of these things then expresses the sense of the proposition.

3.1432   We must not say, "The complex sign '*aRb*' says '*a* stands in relation *R to b*' "; but we must say, "That '*a*' stands in a certain relation to '*b*' says *that aRb*."

3.144   States of affairs can be described but not *named*.

(Names resemble points: propositions resemble arrows, they have sense.)

3.2   In propositions thoughts can be so expressed that to the objects of the thoughts correspond the elements of the propositional sign.

3.201   These elements I call "simple signs" and the proposition "completely analysed."

3.202   The simple signs employed in propositions are called names.

3.203   The name means the object. The object is its meaning. ("*A*" is the same sign as "*A*.")

. . . a man can do as he will, but not will as he will.

—*Arthur Schopenhauer*

William Blake was a visionary poet and painter who lived in Britain in the late 1700s. He was largely unappreciated and misunderstood during his lifetime. One of Blake's contemporaries even referred to him as a harmless lunatic. Blake spent his life not only as a dedicated husband and well-regarded engraver but also as a kind of mystic—claiming to receive messages from the dead and see ghosts. Modern scholars consider Blake to be a genius, and modern students often find his work puzzling.

Blake wrote and illustrated his own poetry books, using the same skills in his profession as an engraver. When Blake died, he was buried in an unmarked grave at a public cemetery in London. After his death, the English poet William Wordsworth remarked that "There was no doubt that this poor man was mad, but there is something in the madness of this man which interests me more than the sanity of Lord Byron and Walter Scott."

Blake explores the coexistence of good and evil in the universe through Romantic ideas of innocence and experience. In his poem "The Tyger," Blake considers a god who would create a creature with such deadly natural impulses that it would destroy his other creation, the lamb.

William Blake

"The Tyger"

Tyger Tyger, burning bright,
In the forests of the night:
What immortal hand or eye,
Could frame thy fearful symmetry?

In what distant deeps or skies
Burnt the fire of thine eyes!
On what wings dare he aspire?
What the hand, dare sieze the fire?

And what shoulder, & what art,
Could twist the sinews of thy heart?
And when thy heart began to beat,
What dread hand? & what dread feet?

What the hammer? what the chain,
In what furnace was thy brain?
What the anvil? what dread grasp,
Dare its deadly terror clasp?

When the stars threw down their spears
And water'd heaven with their tears:

Did he smile his work to see?
Did he who made the Lamb make thee?

Tyger, Tyger burning bright,
In the forests of the night:
What immortal hand or eye,
Dare frame thy fearful symmetry?

Born in 1923, Ian Barbour is an American theologian and physicist who in 1999 won the Templeton Prize for Progress in Religion. Despite becoming a distinguished physics professor in his twenties, Barbour went on to study theology and ethics at Yale Divinity School and began exploring the relationship between science and religion, a field in which he is now recognized as a leading authority.

In *When Science Meets Religion*, Barbour addresses ideas of religious and scientific determinism, two subjects that have generally been at odds with each other since the 1700s.

Ian Barbour

from *When Science Meets Religion*

CONFLICT

Biblical literalism did not lead to conflicts with Newtonian physics like those that occurred with Copernican astronomy or Darwinian evolution. But in the centuries following Newton, the idea of a universe rigidly determined by natural laws seemed incompatible with traditional ideas of God's action in the world. More recently, the role of chance in quantum phenomena has challenged ideas of divine purpose and sovereignty.

The conflicts with religion arising in the history of physics may not have been as dramatic as those arising from astronomy or evolution, but they have been important because physics has been viewed as the most fundamental of the sciences. The most significant conflict has involved the relation between God's control of events, determination by natural laws, and the presence of chance at the quantum level.

1. God in a Deterministic World

Newtonian physics did not at first seem to present any challenge to religious beliefs. Almost all of the scientists of the seventeenth century were devout Christians. Newton himself believed that God keeps the stars from collapsing under gravitational attraction and intervenes periodically to correct planetary perturbations in the solar system (perturbations that Pierre Laplace later showed would eventually cancel each other out). But Newton and his contemporaries saw God's hand mainly in the harmonious design of the universe. In their view, the world is an intricate machine following immutable laws, but it expresses the wisdom of an intelligent creator.

Moreover, God was held to have an ongoing role in a *law-abiding world*. God not only designed the laws but sustains them continually. The laws are a continuing expression of God's purposes and sovereignty. God predestines and foresees all events; everything that happens is in accordance with God's will. Newtonian scientists held that the passivity of matter in their science is consistent with traditional ideas of God's sovereignty and transcendence and is inconsistent with pantheism, astrology, vitalism, and alchemy, in which matter itself was held to be more active. Newtonians agreed with medieval philosophers that God as "primary cause" makes use of the "secondary causes" described by science as instruments to achieve predetermined purposes.

But during the eighteenth century, traditional theism often gave way to *deism:* the belief that God started the universe and left it to run by itself. In a clockwork world, God's role was restricted to that of clockmaker. The argument from design (natural theology) was initially advanced to support revealed theology, but before long it was taken as a substitute for the latter. What started as reinterpretation within a Christian community rooted in scripture and personal religious experience often ended with a distant and impersonal God. Especially among the Enlightenment philosophers in France, a stronger hostility to the church and all forms of religion developed. A militant atheism was advanced in the name of science, accompanied by great confidence in the power of reason and human progress.

Newton's laws of motion and gravity seemed to govern all objects, from the smallest particle to the most distant planet. The concepts of Newtonian physics were spectacularly successful in explaining a wide range of phenomena, and it is understandable that it was assumed that they could explain *all* events. They were extended to form an all-encompassing metaphysics of *materialism* defended by some of the philosophers of the Enlightenment. *Determinism* was most explicitly defended by Laplace, who claimed that if we knew the position and velocity of every particle in the universe, we could calculate all future events. His claim is *reductionist* in assuming that the behavior of all entities is determined by the behavior of their smallest components. When Napoleon said to him, "M. Laplace, they tell me that you have written this large book on the system of the universe, and have never mentioned its Creator," Laplace gave his famous reply: "I have no need of that hypothesis."

2. God and Chance

Of the three interpretations of the uncertainties present in quantum theory outlined earlier in this chapter, the first maintains that the world itself is completely *determined*, even though we have not yet found all its exact laws. Einstein, the most prominent defender of this view, believed that there are hidden variables we have yet to discover. The second view ascribes uncertainty to inescapable experimental or conceptual limitations, and it remains *agnostic* about what is going on in the world apart from us. Bohr has commonly been associated with this view. The third view, which Heisenberg advocated, defends *indeterminacy* in nature. The atomic world contains a range of potentialities. The realization of a particular observation or event within a given probability distribution is entirely a matter of chance.

In itself, chance is *random*, whereas divine action is said to be purposeful and goal-directed. Some writers hold that the presence of chance undermines theistic beliefs and supports a materialistic philosophy. Earlier in the century, Bertrand Russell wrote, "Man is the product of causes which had no prevision of the end they were achieving; his origin, his growth, his hopes and fears, his loves and his beliefs, are but the outcome of accidental collocations of atoms." In the previous chapter we saw that some cosmologists have proposed theories postulating many universes (whether in the form of successive cycles of expansion and contraction, isolated domains, Everett's "many worlds," or multiple quantum vacuum fluctuations). The fundamental constants might vary among these universes, and we just happen by chance to live in one that is just right for the emergence of life and consciousness. These cosmologists believe that our existence is the product of chance and not purpose.

Jacques Monod maintains in *Chance and Necessity* that the presence of chance in nature supports materialism and excludes a theistic interpretation. He writes primarily about evolutionary biology, in which chance and necessity are represented by random mutations and natural selection, but he gives examples from other fields of science. He says that the prevalence of chance shows that this is a purposeless universe. "Man knows that he is alone in the universe's immensity, out of which he emerged only by chance." Chance is "the source of all novelty, all creation." Monod holds that all phenomena can be reduced to the laws of physics and chemistry and the operation of chance. "Anything can be reduced to simple, obvious mechanical interactions. The cell is a machine. The animal is a machine. Man is a machine."

There are two possible theological responses to indeterminacy at the quantum level. The first is to say that the choice among the range of possibilities left open by quantum theory is *not a matter of chance*, but is made by God without violating natural laws and without being scientifically detectable. The laws of nature specify only a range of potentialities, but God determines which one is actually realized. The "hidden variable" is God, not a still undiscovered deeper level of deterministic laws. This position is explored in the last section of this chapter.

The second theological response is to assert that *both law and chance are part of God's design*. The biochemist and theologian Arthur Peacocke gives chance a positive role in the exploration of the potentialities inherent in the created order. This approach is consistent with the idea of divine purpose, though not with the idea of a precise predetermined plan. Through the built-in potentialities of higher levels of organization, God could envision a general direction of evolutionary change but not the exact sequence of events. This proposal is explored in the next chapter (see "God and Continuing Creation"). In Chapter 6 we will meet other writers who suggest that the acknowledgment of law and chance (along with waste, evil, and suffering) in nature should lead us to modify or reject classical ideas of divine omnipotence (see "God's Self-Limitation" and "Process Theology").

INDEPENDENCE

Two ideas taken from interpretations of quantum physics have been used to defend the independence of science and religion. First, an *instrumentalist* account of quantum theories can be combined with an instrumentalist account of religious beliefs to argue that science and the genetic tendencies inherited from our prehuman and Stone Age ancestors.

Rolston gives particular attention to the *evolution of morality*. He holds that terms such as *selfish genes* and *altruism* in lower life forms are misleading metaphors because at those levels there are no moral agents with the capacity for choice. He claims that the capacity for morality, but not particular moral judgments, is the product of natural selection—just as there is a genetic basis for the capacity for language but not for particular languages, or a genetic basis for the capacity to reason but not for particular rational arguments. He finds implausible the claims that all human altruism is really covert self-interest or the expectation of future reciprocation or social approval. Such explanations simply do not fit the Good Samaritan in the biblical story, or the life of Mother Teresa, or the person who saves the life of a drowning stranger.

Rolston points out that the sociobiologists themselves subscribe to values that cannot be justified by their own theories. It seems implausible that Wilson's deep concern for endangered species, for example, is only an unconscious and indirect way of maximizing his own genetic fitness. Rolston maintains that the capacity for moral judgment is a product of evolutionary history, but he holds that we must turn to philosophy and theology for the grounds of moral judgments. Rolston's view of the evolution of morality is compatible with Christian views of human nature, whereas Wilson's is not.

3. Genetic Determinism and Human Freedom

Behavioral genetics studies the correlation of genes with behavior in the present rather than in evolutionary history. It has sometimes been claimed that our fate is determined by our genes, or that a person cannot be held responsible for a violent act because "his genes made him do it." Studies of identical twins suggest that for many behavioral traits genetic factors account for roughly half of the variation. In one study comparing the brothers of 161 gay men, 52 percent of identical twins (sharing all their genes) were also gay, but only 22 percent of fraternal twins and 11 percent of adopted brothers were also gay. A study of adopted children found that 2.9 percent had criminal records if neither biological nor adoptive parents had criminal records, 6.7 percent if only biological parents had such records, 12.1 percent if only adoptive parents did, and 40 percent if both sets of parents did.

Other studies report that the percentage of Afro-Americans in prison is nine times that of the white population, and some commentators have concluded that *genetic differences* are responsible for criminal behavior. But this interpretation is highly questionable. Most if not all of the racial differences in prison rates can be attributed not to genetic but to social factors, such as higher unemployment among Afro-Americans and discrimination in arrest and conviction rates (which are six times higher than for others for comparable crimes). Controversial genetic studies have often been publicized by the media without the qualifications expressed in the original reports; likewise, later studies failing to confirm the initial reports have seldom been publicized. Studies of alcoholism are particularly problematic because alcoholism seems to have several forms, each of which is affected by many genes as well as by personal history and cultural environment. Genetic and cultural factors cannot be separated in any simple way, because even twins may seek out different environments, subcultures, and experiences that in turn affect their lives. Nature and nurture are always present together, and neither can be considered in isolation.

But even if we allow for the influence of environment as well as genes, we still have not allowed for *human freedom*. Severe constraints are indeed imposed by nature and nurture. Genes establish a range of potentials and predispositions. Parents and social institutions present us with acceptable patterns of behavior. Freedom does not mean that our actions are uncaused or indeterminate, but rather that they are the result of our motives, intentions, and choices and are not externally coerced. Freedom is self-determination at the level of the person. We are not passive stimulus-response mechanisms but selves who can envision novel possibilities and decide deliberately and responsibly among alternative actions. In the case of well-established habits, changes are not easily made, but they can occur if a person seeks a supportive context, as twelve-step programs for alcoholism have shown. We cannot choose the cards we have been dealt, but we can to some extent choose what we do with them.

While we may be only partially controlled by our genes from the past, we know also that the science of genetics will give us new powers over human life in the future. Some religious leaders are opposed to all *genetic intervention* or *genetic engineering*. They claim that to "tamper with DNA," especially in an attempt to alter human nature, would be "playing God" and transgressing our limits. We will lose reverence for life, they say, if we seek God-like powers to redesign it. Manipulation of genes is said to be another form of technocratic arrogance like that portrayed in the myth of Prometheus, the story of the tower of Babel, and the modern novel about Dr. Frankenstein. I suggest, however, that differing views of genetic intervention do not represent a conflict between science and religion as systems of belief, but rather a conflict between differing ethical judgments about the applications of science. Instead of rejecting all forms of genetic intervention, we need to make distinctions among them.

Many authors have maintained that modification of *somatic cells* (body cells that are not passed on to future generations) should be distinguished from modification of *germ cells* (reproductive cells that *are* passed on). The latter modification would have more long-lasting effects but also greater risks of uncertain and perhaps irreversible consequences. Moreover, intervention aimed at *preventing genetic defects* (particularly those resulting in debilitating or fatal diseases, such as Huntington's disease or cystic fibrosis) should be distinguished from intervention aimed at *enhancing particular traits* (such as intelligence, height, or physical strength). The latter is more dubious scientifically (since most traits depend on many interacting genes rather than a single gene) and also more dubious ethically (since it would perpetuate the cultural biases and personal preferences of particular parents or societies). The line between prevention and enhancement is of course not a sharp one, but the motives are likely to be rather different.

A final distinction must be made between intervention in *human* and *nonhuman* life. The cloning of Dolly, the Scottish sheep whose genes were identical with its mother's, was motivated by the hope of producing proteins for the treatment of human diseases. It is a very different matter when someone proposes using what are still high-risk techniques so that people can have themselves cloned. The human clone and the human gene donor would of course differ more than identical twins because they would grow up in differing generations and environments. But human cloning, like gene modification to enhance traits, would treat people as objects to be manipulated or products to be redesigned. Such measures would put a heavy burden of expectation on the newborn child. The search for a "perfect" child might also change our attitudes toward people with genetic disabilities. The Christian tradition holds that God's love and acceptance of each person is unconditional, and that ours should be also. In any case, the discussion of ethical decisions about the uses of our new genetic knowledge is an expression of our human freedom, which implies the rejection of both evolutionary and behavioral genetic determinism.

Thomas Hardy was born in Dorset in 1840. His physical frailty delayed his attendance at school until he was about eight years old. At sixteen, Hardy became the apprentice to an architect, and he eventually moved to London. However, poor health soon compelled him to return to the Dorset country air. He married when he was thirty-four to Emma Gifford, who encouraged Hardy's literary pursuits. Hardy's novels include *Far from the Madding Crowd*, *Tess of the D'urbervilles*, and *Jude the Obscure*—which caused a great deal of controversy among the conservative members of Victorian Britain. In 1912, Hardy's wife died, and some of Hardy's most interesting work expresses his complicated feelings toward her. Two years after her death, Hardy married his secretary. He died in 1928, and although his living wish was to be buried beside his first wife, he was interred at Poet's Corner in Westminster Abbey, London—while his heart was buried near Emma Hardy's grave.

In *Jude the Obscure*, Hardy tells the story of a young man who never quite finds the door that leads to his imagined destiny. In the early part of the book, Jude hastily gets married to a woman whom he believes is carrying his child. It turns out, however, that she is not pregnant, and Jude finds himself trapped in a marriage with someone who doesn't understand him. No matter what Jude decides to do, his suffering seems unavoidable.

Thomas Hardy

from *Jude the Obscure*

X

The time arrived for killing the pig which Jude and his wife had fattened in their sty during the autumn months, and the butchering was timed to take place as soon as it was light in the morning, so that Jude might get to Alfredston without losing more than a quarter of a day.

The night had seemed strangely silent. Jude looked out of the window long before dawn, and perceived that the ground was covered with snow—snow rather deep for the season, it seemed, a few flakes still falling.

"I'm afraid the pig-killer won't be able to come," he said to Arabella.

"O, he'll come. You must get up and make the water hot, if you want Challow to scald him. Though I like singeing best."

"I'll get up," said Jude. "I like the way of my own county."

He went downstairs, lit the fire under the copper, and began feeding it with bean-stalks, all the time without a candle, the blaze flinging a cheerful shine into the room; though for him the sense of cheerfulness was lessened by thoughts on the reason of that blaze—to heat water to scald an animal that as yet lived, and whose voice could be continually heard from a corner of the garden. At half-past six, the time of appointment with the butcher, the water boiled, and Jude's wife came downstairs.

"Is Challow come?" she asked.

"No."

They waited, and it grew lighter, with the dreary light of a snowy dawn. She went out, gazed along the road, and returning said, "He's not coming. Drunk last night, I expect. The snow is not enough to hinder him, surely!"

"Then we must put it off. It is only the water boiled for nothing. The snow may be deep in the valley."

"Can't be put off. There's no more victuals for the pig. He ate the last mixing o' barleymeal yesterday morning."

"Yesterday morning? What has he lived on since?"

"Nothing."

"What—he has been starving?"

"Yes. We always do it the last day or two, to save bother with the innerds. What ignorance, not to know that!"

"That accounts for his crying so. Poor creature!"

"Well—you must do the sticking—there's no help for it. I'll show you how. Or I'll do it myself—I think I could. Though as it is such a big pig I had rather Challow had done it. However, his basket o' knives and things have been already sent on here, and we can use 'em."

"Of course you shan't do it," said Jude. "I'll do it, since it must be done."

He went out to the sty, shovelled away the snow for the space of a couple of yards or more, and placed the stool in front, with the knives and ropes at hand. A robin peered down at the preparations from the nearest tree, and, not liking the sinister look of the scene, flew away, though hungry. By this time Arabella had joined her husband, and Jude, rope in hand, got into the sty, and noosed the affrighted animal, who, beginning with a squeak of surprise, rose to repeated cries of rage. Arabella opened the sty-door, and together they hoisted the victim on to the stool, legs upward, and while Jude held him Arabella bound him down, looping the cord over his legs to keep him from struggling.

The animal's note changed its quality. It was not now rage, but the cry of despair; long-drawn, slow and hopeless.

"Upon my soul I would sooner have gone without the pig than have had this to do!" said Jude. "A creature I have fed with my own hands."

"Don't be such a tender-hearted fool! There's the sticking-knife—the one with the point. Now whatever you do, don't stick un too deep."

"I'll stick un effectually, so as to make short work of it. That's the chief thing."

"You must not!" she cried. "The meat must be well bled, and to do that he must die slow. We shall lose a shilling a score if the meat is red and bloody! Just touch the vein, that's all. I was brought up to it, and I know. Every good butcher keeps un bleeding long. He ought to be eight or ten minutes dying, at least."

"He shall not be half a minute if I can help it, however the meat may look," said Jude determinedly. Scraping the bristles from the pig's upturned throat, as he had seen the butchers do, he slit the fat; then plunged in the knife with all his might.

"'Od damn it all!" she cried, "that ever I should say it! You've over-stuck un! And I telling you all the time—"

"Do be quiet, Arabella, and have a little pity on the creature!"

However unworkmanlike the deed, it had been mercifully done. The blood flowed out in a torrent instead of in the trickling stream she had desired. The dying animal's cry assumed its third and final tone, the shriek of agony; his glazing eyes rivetting themselves on Arabella with the eloquently keen reproach of a creature recognizing at last the treachery of those who had seemed his only friends.

"Make un stop that!" said Arabella. "Such a noise will bring somebody or other up here, and I don't want people to know we are doing it ourselves." Picking up the knife from the ground whereon Jude had flung it, she slipped it into the gash, and slit the wind-pipe. The pig was instantly silent, his dying breath coming through the hole.

"That's better," she said.

SIMON VAN BOOY

"It is a hateful business!" said he.

"Pigs must be killed."

The animal heaved in a final convulsion, and, despite the rope, kicked out with all his last strength. A tablespoonful of black chat came forth, the trickling of red blood having ceased for some seconds.

"That's it; now he'll go," said she. "Artful creatures—they always keep back a drop like that as long as they can!"

The last plunge had come so unexpectedly as to make Jude stagger, and in recovering himself he kicked over the vessel in which the blood had been caught.

"There!" she cried, thoroughly in a passion. "Now I can't make any blackpot. There's a waste, all through you!"

Jude put the pan upright, but only about a third of the whole steaming liquid was left in it, the main part being splashed over the snow, and forming a dismal, sordid, ugly spectacle—to those who saw it as other than an ordinary obtaining of meat. The lips and nostrils of the animal turned livid, then white, and the muscles of his limbs relaxed.

"Thank God!" Jude said. "He's dead."

"What's God got to do with such a messy job as a pig-killing. I should like to know!" she said scornfully. "Poor folks must live."

"I know, I know," said he. "I don't scold you."

Suddenly they became aware of a voice at hand.

"Well done, young married volk! I couldn't have carried it out much better myself, cuss me if I could!" The voice, which was husky, came from the garden-gate, and looking up from the scene of slaughter they saw the burly form of Mr. Challow leaning over the gate, critically surveying their performance.

"'Tis well for 'ee to stand there and glane!" said Arabella. "Owing to your being late the meat is blooded and half spoiled! 'Twon't fetch so much by a shilling a score!"

Challow expressed his contrition. "You should have waited a bit," he said, shaking his head, "and not have done this—in the delicate state, too, that you be in at present, ma'am. 'Tis risking yourself too much."

"You needn't be concerned about that," said Arabella, laughing. Jude too laughed, but there was a strong flavour of bitterness in his amusement.

Challow made up for his neglect of the killing by zeal in the scalding and scraping. Jude felt dissatisfied with himself as a man at what he had done, though aware of his lack of common sense, and that the deed would have amounted to the same thing if carried out by deputy. The white snow, stained with the blood of his fellow-mortal, wore an illogical look to him as a lover of justice, not to say a Christian; but he could not see how the matter was to be mended. No doubt he was, as his wife had called him, a tender-hearted fool.

He did not like the road to Alfredston now. It stared him cynically in the face. The wayside objects reminded him so much of his courtship of his wife that, to keep them out of his eyes, he read whenever he could as he walked to and from his work. Yet he sometimes felt that by caring for books he was not escaping commonplace nor gaining rare ideas, every working-man being of that taste now. When passing near the spot by the stream on which he had first made her acquaintance he one day heard voices just as he had done at that earlier time. One of the girls who had been Arabella's companions was talking to a friend in a shed, himself being the subject of discourse, possibly because they had seen him in the distance. They were quite unaware that the shed-walls were so thin that he could hear their words as he passed.

"Howsomever, 'twas I put her up to it! 'Nothing venture nothing have,' I said. If I hadn't she'd no more have been his mis'ess than I."

"'Tis my belief she knew before . . ."

What had Arabella been put up to by this woman, so that he should make her his "mis'ess," otherwise wife? The suggestion was horridly unpleasant, and it rankled in his mind so much that instead of entering his own cottage when he reached it he flung his basket inside the garden-gate and passed on, determined to go and see his old aunt and get some supper there.

This made his arrival home rather late. Arabella, however, was busy melting down lard from fat of the deceased pig, for she had been out on a jaunt all day, and so delayed her work. Dreading lest what he had heard should lead him to say something regrettable to her he spoke little. But Arabella was very talkative, and said among other things that she wanted some money. Seeing the book sticking out of his pocket she added that he ought to earn more.

"An apprentice's wages are not meant to be enough to keep a wife on, as a rule, my dear."

"Then you shouldn't have had one."

"Come, Arabella! That's too bad, when you know how it came about."

"I'll declare afore Heaven that I thought what I told you was true. Doctor Vilbert thought so. It was a good job for you that it wasn't so!"

"I don't mean that," he said hastily. "I mean before that time. I know it was not your fault; but those women friends of yours gave you bad advice. If they hadn't, or you hadn't taken it, we should at this moment have been free from a bond which, not to mince matters, galls both of us devilishly. It may be very sad, but it is true."

"Who's been telling you about my friends? What advice? I insist upon your telling me."

"Pooh—I'd rather not."

"But you shall—you ought to. It is mean 'ee not to!"

"Very well." And he hinted gently what had been revealed to him. "But I don't wish to dwell upon it. Let us say no more about it."

Her defensive manner collapsed. "That was nothing," she said, laughing coldly. "Every woman has a right to do such as that. The risks is hers."

"I quite deny it, Bella. She might if no life-long penalty attached to it for the man, or, in his default, for herself if the weakness of the moment could end with the moment, or even with the year. But when effects stretch so far she should not go and do that which entraps a man if he is honest, or herself if he is otherwise."

"What ought I to have done?"

"Given me time . . . Why do you fuss yourself about melting down that pig's fat tonight? Please put it away!"

"Then I must do it tomorrow morning. It won't keep."

"Very well—do."

XI

Next morning, which was Sunday, she resumed operations about ten o'clock, and the renewed work recalled the conversation which had accompanied it the night before, and put her back into the same intractable temper.

"That's the story about me in Marygreen, is it—that I entrapped 'ee? Much of a catch you was, Lord send!" As she warmed she saw some of Jude's dear ancient classics on a table where they ought not to have been laid. "I won't have them books here in the way!" she cried petulantly, and seizing them one by one she began throwing them upon the floor.

"Leave my books alone!" he said. "You might have thrown them aside if you had liked, but as to soiling them like that, it is disgusting!" In the operation of making lard Arabella's hands had become smeared with the hot grease, and her fingers consequently left very perceptible imprints on the book-covers. She continued deliberately to toss the books severally upon the floor, till Jude, incensed beyond bearing, caught her by the arms to make her leave off. Somehow, in doing so, he loosened the fastening of her hair, and it rolled about her ears.

"Let me go!" she said.

"Promise to leave the books alone."

She hesitated. "Let me go!" she repeated.

"Promise!"

After a pause: "I do."

Jude relinquished his hold, and she crossed the room to the door, out of which she went with a set face, and into the highway. Here she began to saunter up and down, perversely pulling her hair into a worse disorder than he had caused, and unfastening several buttons of her gown. It was a fine Sunday morning, dry, clear and frosty, and the bells of Alfredston Church could be heard on the breeze from the north. People were going along the road, dressed in their holiday clothes: they were mainly lovers—such pairs as Jude and Arabella had been when they sported along the same track some months earlier. These pedestrians turned to stare at the extraordinary spectacle she now presented, bonnetless, her dishevelled hair blowing in the wind, her bodice apart. her sleeves rolled above her elbows for her work, and her hands reeking with melted fat. One of the passers said in mock terror:

"Good Lord deliver us!"

"See how he's served me!" she cried. "Making me work Sunday mornings when I ought to be going to my church, and tearing my hair off my head, and my gown off my back!"

Jude was exasperated and went out to drag her in by main force. Then he suddenly lost his heat. Illuminated with the sense that all was over between them, and that it mattered not what she did, or he, her husband stood still, regarding her. Their lives were ruined, he thought; ruined by the fundamental error of their matrimonial union; that of having based a permanent contract on a temporary feeling which had no necessary connection with affinities that alone render a life-long comradeship tolerable.

"Going to ill-use me on principle as your father ill-used your mother and your father's sister ill-used her husband?" she asked. "All you be a queer lot as husbands and wives!"

Jude fixed an arrested, surprised look on her. But she said no more and continued her saunter till she was tired. He left the spot, and after wandering vaguely a little while, walked in the direction of Marygreen. Here he called upon his great-aunt, whose infirmities daily increased.

"Aunt—did my father ill-use my mother, and my aunt her husband?" said Jude abruptly, sitting down by the fire.

She raised her ancient eyes under the rim of the bygone bonnet that she always wore. "Who's been telling you that?" she said.

"I have heard it spoken of, and want to know all."

"You med so well, I s'pose; though your wife—I reckon 'twas she—must have been a fool to open up that! There isn't much to know after all. Your father and mother couldn't get on together, and they parted. It was coming home from Al-fredston market, when you were a baby—on the hill by the Brown House barn—that they had their last difference, and took leave of one another for the last time. Your mother soon afterwards died—she drowned herself, in short, and your father went away with you to South Wessex, and never came here any more."

Jude recalled his father's silence about North Wessex and

Jude's mother, never speaking of either till his dying day.

"It was the same with your father's sister. Her husband offended her, and she so disliked living with him afterwards that she went away to London with her little maid. The Fawleys were not made for wedlock, it never seemed to sit well upon us. There's sommat in our blood that won't take kindly to the notion of being bound to do what we do readily enough if not bound. That's why you ought to have hearkened to me, and not ha' married."

"Where did father and mother part—by the Brown House, did you say?"

"A little further on—where the road to Fenworth branches off, and the handpost stands. A gibbet once stood there."

In the dusk of that evening Jude walked away from his old aunt's as if to go home. But as soon as he reached the open down he struck out upon it till he came to a large round pond. The frost continued, though it was not particularly sharp, and the larger stars overhead came out slow and flickering. Jude put one foot on the edge of the ice, and then the other; it cracked under his weight: but this did not deter him. He ploughed his way inward to the centre, the ice making sharp noises as he went. When just about the middle he looked around him and gave a jump. The cracking repeated itself; but he did not go down. He jumped again, but the cracking had ceased. Jude went back to the edge, and stepped upon the ground.

It was curious, he thought. What was he reserved for? He supposed he was not a sufficiently dignified person for suicide. Peaceful death abhorred him as a subject, and would not take him.

What could he do of a lower kind than self-extermination: what was there less noble, more in keeping with his present degraded position? He could get drunk. Of course that was it: he had forgotten. Drinking was the regular, stereotyped resource of the despairing worthless. He began to see now why some men boozed at inns. He struck down the hill northwards and came to an obscure public-house. On entering and sitting down the sight of the picture of Samson and Delilah on the wall caused him to recognize the place as that he had visited with Arabella on that first Sunday evening of their courtship. He called for liquor and drank briskly for an hour or more.

Staggering homeward late that night, with all his sense of depression gone, and his head fairly clear still, he began to laugh boisterously and to wonder how Arabella would receive him in his new aspect. The house was in darkness when he entered, and in his stumbling state it was some time before he could get a light. Then he found that though the mark of pig-dressing, of fats and scallops, were visible, the materials themselves had been taken away. A line written by his wife on the inside of an old envelope was pinned to the cotton blower of the fireplace:

"*Have gone to my friends. Shall not return.*"

All the next day he remained at home, and sent off the car-case of the pig to Alfredston. He then cleaned up the premises, locked the door, put the key in a place she would know if she came back and returned to his masonry at Alfredston.

At night when he again plodded home he found she had not visited the house. The next day went in the same way, and the next. Then there came a letter from her.

That she had grown tired of him she frankly admitted. He was such a slow old coach, and she did not care for the sort of life he led. There was no prospect of his ever bettering himself or her. She further went on to say that her parents had, as he knew, for some time considered the question of emigrating to Australia, the pig-jobbing business being a poor one nowa-days. They had at last decided to go and she proposed to go with them, if he had no objection. A woman of her sort would have more chance over there than in this stupid country.

Jude replied that he had not the least objection to her going. He thought it a wise course, since she wished to go, and one that might be to the advantage of both. He enclosed in the packet containing the letter the money that had been realized by the sale of the pig, with all he had besides, which was not much.

From that day he heard no more of her except indirectly, though her father and his household did not immediately leave, but waited till his goods and other effects had been sold off. When Jude learnt that there was to be an auction at the house of the Donns he packed his own household goods into a waggon, and sent them to her at the aforesaid homestead, that she might sell them with the rest, or as many of them as she should choose.

He then went into lodgings at Alfredston, and saw in a shop-window the little handbill announcing the sale of his father-in law's furniture. He noted its date, which came and passed without Jude's going near the place, or perceiving that the traffic out of Alfredston by the southern road was materially increased by the auction. A few days later he entered a little broker's shop in the main street of the town, and amid a heterogeneous collection of saucepans, a clothes-horse, rolling pin, brass candlestick, swing looking-glass, and other things at the back of the shop, evidently just brought in from a sale, he perceived a little framed photograph, which turned out to be his own portrait.

It was one which he had had specially taken and framed by a local man in bird's-eye maple, as a present for Arabella, and had duly given her on their wedding-day. On the back was still to be read, *"Jude to Arabella,"* with the date. She must have thrown it in with the rest of her property at the auction.

"Oh," said the broker, seeing him look at this and the other articles in the heap, and not perceiving that the portrait was of himself: "It is a small lot of stuff that was knocked down to me at a cottage sale out on the road to Marygreen. The frame is a very useful one, if you take out the likeness. You shall have it for a shilling."

The utter death of every tender sentiment in his wife, as brought home to him by this mute and undesigned evidence of her sale of his portrait and gift, was the conclusive little stroke required to demolish all sentiment in him. He paid the shilling, took the photograph away with him, and burnt it, frame and all, when he reached his lodging.

Two or three days later he heard that Arabella and her parents had departed. He had sent a message offering to see her for a formal leave-taking, but she had said that it would be better otherwise, since she was bent on going, which perhaps was true. On the evening following their emigration, when his day's work was done, he came out of doors after supper, and strolled in the starlight along the too familiar road towards the upland whereon had been experienced the chief emotions of his life. It seemed to be his own again.

He could not realize himself. On the old track he seemed to be a boy still, hardly a day older than when he had stood dreaming at the top of that hill, inwardly fired for the first time with ardours for Christminster and scholarship. "Yet I am a man," he said. "I have a wife. More, I have arrived at the still riper stage of having disagreed with her, disliked her, had a scuffle with her, and parted from her."

He remembered then that he was standing not far from the spot at which the parting between his father and his mother was said to have occurred.

A little further on was the summit, whence Christminster, or what he had taken for that city, had seemed to be visible. A milestone now as always, stood at the roadside hard by. Jude drew near it, and felt rather than read the mileage to the city. He remembered that once on his way home he had proudly cut with his keen new chisel an inscription on the back of that milestone, embodying his aspirations. It had been done in the first week of his apprenticeship, before he had been diverted from his purposes by an unsuitable woman. He wondered if the inscription were legible still, and going to the back of the milestone brushed away the nettles. By the light of a match he could still discern what he had cut so enthusiastically so long ago.

THITHER

J. F.

The sight of it, unimpaired, within its screen of grass and net-tles, lit in his soul a spark of the old fire. Surely his plan should be to move onward through good and ill—to avoid morbid

SIMON VAN BOOY

sorrow even though he did see uglinesses in the world? *Bene agere et latari*—to do good cheerfully—which he had heard to be the philosophy of one Spinoza, might be his own even now.

He might battle with his evil star, and follow out his original intention.

By moving to a spot a little way off he uncovered the horizon in a north-easterly direction. There actually rose the faint halo, a small dim nebulousness, hardly recognizable save by the eye of faith. It was enough for him. He would go to Christ-minster as soon as the term of his apprenticeship expired.

He returned to his lodgings in a better mood, and said his prayers.

One of the most popular stories about inevitable suffering comes from the Old Testament of the Holy Bible.

Genesis 2:7–3:24 from the Holy Bible

2:7: And the Lord God formed man of the dust of the ground, and breathed into his nostrils the breath of life; and man became a living soul.

2:8: And the Lord God planted a garden eastward in Eden; and there he put the man whom he had formed.

2:9: And out of the ground made the Lord God to grow every tree that is pleasant to the sight, and good for food; the tree of life also in the midst of the garden, and the tree of knowledge of good and evil.

2:10: And a river went out of Eden to water the garden; and from thence it was parted, and became into four heads.

2:11: The name of the first is Pison: that is it which compasseth the whole land of Havilah, where there is gold;

2:12: And the gold of that land is good: there is bdellium and the onyx stone.

2:13: And the name of the second river is Gihon: the same is it that compasseth the whole land of Ethiopia.

2:14: And the name of the third river is Hiddekel: that is it which goeth toward the east of Assyria. And the fourth river is Euphrates.

2:15: And the Lord God took the man, and put him into the garden of Eden to dress it and to keep it.

2:16: And the Lord God commanded the man, saying, Of every tree of the garden thou mayest freely eat:

2:17: But of the tree of the knowledge of good and evil, thou shalt not eat of it: for in the day that thou eatest thereof thou shalt surely die.

2:18: And the Lord God said, It is not good that the man should be alone; I will make him an help meet for him.

2:19: And out of the ground the Lord God formed every beast of the field, and every fowl of the air; and brought them unto Adam to see what he would call them: and whatsoever Adam called every living creature, that was the name thereof.

2:20: And Adam gave names to all cattle, and to the fowl of the air, and to every beast of the field; but for Adam there was not found an help meet for him.

2:21: And the Lord God caused a deep sleep to fall upon Adam and he slept: and he took one of his ribs, and closed up the flesh instead thereof;

2:22: And the rib, which the Lord God had taken from man, made he a woman, and brought her unto the man.

2:23: And Adam said, This is now bone of my bones, and flesh of my flesh: she shall be called Woman, because she was taken out of Man.

2:24: Therefore shall a man leave his father and his mother, and shall cleave unto his wife: and they shall be one flesh.

SIMON VAN BOOY

2:25: And they were both naked, the man and his wife, and were not ashamed.

3:1: Now the serpent was more subtil than any beast of the field which the Lord God had made. And he said unto the woman, Yea, hath God said, Ye shall not eat of every tree of the garden?

3:2: And the woman said unto the serpent, We may eat of the fruit of the trees of the garden:

3:3: But of the fruit of the tree which is in the midst of the garden, God hath said, Ye shall not eat of it, neither shall ye touch it, lest ye die.

3:4: And the serpent said unto the woman, Ye shall not surely die:

3:5: For God doth know that in the day ye eat thereof, then your eyes shall be opened, and ye shall be as gods, knowing good and evil.

3:6: And when the woman saw that the tree was good for food, and that it was pleasant to the eyes, and a tree to be desired to make one wise, she took of the fruit thereof, and did eat, and gave also unto her husband with her; and he did eat.

3:7: And the eyes of them both were opened, and they knew that they were naked; and they sewed fig leaves together, and made themselves aprons.

3:8: And they heard the voice of the Lord God walking in

the garden in the cool of the day: and Adam and his wife hid themselves from the presence of the Lord God amongst the trees of the garden.

3:9:   And the Lord God called unto Adam, and said unto him, Where art thou?

3:10: And he said, I heard thy voice in the garden, and I was afraid, because I was naked; and I hid myself.

3:11: And he said, Who told thee that thou wast naked? Hast thou eaten of the tree, whereof I commanded thee that thou shouldest not eat?

3:12: And the man said, The woman whom thou gavest to be with me, she gave me of the tree, and I did eat.

3:13: And the Lord God said unto the woman, What is this that thou hast done? And the woman said, The serpent beguiled me, and I did eat.

3:14: And the Lord God said unto the serpent, Because thou hast done this, thou art cursed above all cattle, and above every beast of the field; upon thy belly shalt thou go, and dust shalt thou eat all the days of thy life;

3:15: And I will put enmity between thee and the woman, and between thy seed and her seed; it shall bruise thy head, and thou shalt bruise his heel.

ƒ3:17: And unto Adam he said, Because thou hast hearkened unto the voice of thy wife, and hast eaten of the tree, of which I commanded thee, saying, Thou shalt not eat of it;

cursed is the ground for thy sake; in sorrow shalt thou eat of it all the days of thy life;

3:18:   Thorns also and thistles shall it bring forth to thee; and thou shalt eat the herb of the field;

3:19:   In the sweat of thy face shalt thou eat bread, till thou return unto the ground; for out of it wast thou taken: for dust thou art, and unto dust shalt thou return.

3:20:   And Adam called his wife's name Eve: because she was the mother of all living.

3:21:   Unto Adam also and to his wife did the Lord God make coats of skins, and clothed them.

3:22:   And the Lord God said, Behold, the man is become as one of us, to know good and evil: and now, lest he put forth his hand, and take also of the tree of life, and eat, and live for ever:

3:23:   Therefore the Lord God sent him forth from the garden of Eden, to till the ground from whence he was taken.

3:24:   So he drove out the man; and he placed at the east of the garden of Eden Cherubims, and a flaming sword which turned every way, to keep the way of the tree of life.

Albrecht Dürer, *Adam and Eve*, 1504

William Blake

"The Sick Rose"

O Rose thou art sick.
The invisible worm.
That flies in the night
In the howling storm:

Has found out thy bed
Of crimson joy:
And his dark secret love
Does thy life destroy.

We're fools whether we dance or not, so we might as well dance.

—*Japanese Proverb*

If you should have the desire to study Zen under a teacher and see into your own nature, you should first investigate the word shi [death]. If you want to know how to investigate this word, then at all times while walking, standing, sitting, or reclining, without despising activity, without being caught up in quietude, merely investigate the koan: "After you are dead and cremated, where has the main character [chief actor] gone?" Then in a night or two or at most a few days, you will obtain the decisive and ultimate joy.

—*Japanese Zen master Hakuin (1686–1769)*

ACKNOWLEDGMENTS

Amy Baker; Joshua Bodwell; Dr. and Mrs. J. E. Booy; Dr. and Mrs. Raha Booy; Theodore Bouloukos; Douglas and Anita Borroughs, esq.; Milan Bozic; Ken Browar; Bobby Brinson; David Bruson; Dr. S. A. Burgess, academic director and professor at Mediterranean Center for Arts and Sciences; Gabriel Byrne; Tricia Callahan; Michael Colford; Boston Public Library; Christine Corday; Ken and Joann Davis; Justin Dodd; Writing Program at University College Falmouth; Patricio Ferrari; Peggy Flaum; Dr. Giovanni Frazzetto; Colin Gee; Kayleigh George; East Hampton Library; Werner Herzog; Jen Hart; Gregory Henry; Lucas Hunt; Dr. Mickey Kempner;

Alan Kleinberg; Hilary Knight; Bryan LeBoeuf; Eva Lontscharitsch; Alain Malraux; Lisa Mamo; Metropolitan Museum of Art; Metropolitan Opera; MoMA; Dr. Edmund Miller; Cal Morgan; National Gallery, London: Dr. William Neal; New York Society Library; New York School of Visual Arts; Lukas Ortiz; Rogers Memorial Library of Southampton; Jonathan Rabinowitz; Alberto Rojas; Ivan Shaw; Hala Schlub; Philip G. Spitzer; Virginia Stanley; Dolores Henry; the Connolly family; the Gaddis family; the O'Brien family; McNally-Jackson Booksellers; Prairie Lights Books; Shakespeare & Co. Paris; Andy Spade; Anthony Sperdutti; Fred Volkmer; Amy Vreeland; Wim Wenders; Dr. Barbara Wersba; Phaedra Athanasiou at the Brooklyn Academy of Music; and Les Arts Florissants, under the musical direction of William Christie.

I would like to express an even greater debt of gratitude to the following two people:

Carrie Kania, for her brilliance, her vision, her love of Samuel Beckett and Henry Miller, and her unrivaled sense of personal style and her collection of Vivienne Westwood shoes.

My deepest thanks go to Michael Signorelli for his sparkling intelligence, superhuman attention to detail, old-world courtesy, and the fact that he's a fly-fisherman.

PERMISSIONS

Every effort has been made to trace the ownership of copyrighted material and to make full acknowledgment of its use. The editor regrets any errors or omissions, which will be corrected in subsequent editions upon notification in writing to the publisher.

"Missing a Kick," from *Book of Haikus* by Jack Kerouac, edited by Regina Weinreich. © 2003 by the estate of Stella Kerouac; John Sampas, literary representative. Used by permission of Penguin, a division of Penguin Group (USA) Inc. and SLL/Sterling Lord Literistic, Inc.

Excerpts from pp. 70–3, 126–9 from *When Science Meets Religion* by Ian G. Barbour. © 2000 by Ian G. Barbour. Reprinted by permission of HarperCollins Publishers.